NEW YORK CITY
LANDMARKS

NEW YORK CITY
LANDMARKS

Jake Rajs

Text by Francis Morrone

ANTIQUE COLLECTORS' CLUB

To my daughters Chloe and Olivia

Sister Fran, mother Janina

Stepchildren Jack, Sean and Grace

Close friends: Amy, Mark, Jules, Lewis, Tony, Michael, Malcolm, John, Sara,
Francine, Paul, Scott, Steve, Nick, Tim, Bob, Bob, Isaac, and Joe.

Your love, friendship and support have stood the test of time.
You are greatly appreciated.

All photographs in this book are available as fine art prints at
www.jakerajs.com

Images © 2015 Jake Rajs
Text © 2015 Antique Collectors' Club Ltd.
World Copyright Reserved
First published 2012
Second edition 2015

ISBN 978 1 85149 798 0

Every effort has been made to seek permission to reproduce the images in
this book and the authors are grateful to the individuals and institutions
who have assisted in this task. Any errors or omissions are entirely
unintentional, and the details should be addressed to the publisher.

British Library Cataloguing-in-Publication Data
A CIP catalogue record for the book is available from the British Library.

MIX
Paper from
responsible sources
FSC® C104723
FSC
www.fsc.org

Printed and bound in China for
Antique Collectors' Club Ltd, Sandy Lane, Old Martlesham,
Woodbridge, Suffolk, IP12 4SD

Preface

As a young child, I was inspired when I came to New York City on a ship from Israel, like many other immigrants. We arrived in the evening and all the people went on deck to see the Statue of Liberty. People wept with joy. The next morning, I got up at sunrise and went on deck. The wonder of watching the sun's rays hit the tall buildings turning them golden has never left me. Then as now, people come to New York to fulfill their dreams.

I have been a photographer for over 40 years, and have been privileged to have my work take me around America and the world. New York City is my favorite place to photograph; each day there is something new to see and experience in the greatest city in the world. Photography is about editing; to expose what you want out of infinite possibilities. I have created over 300,000 photographs of the city. I am pleased to have narrowed it down so I can share some of my favorite images and places in the city with you in this book.

When I go out to create photographs of architecture, I try to keep in mind what Le Corbusier said: "Light creates ambiance and feel of a place, as well as the expression of a structure." That is why I photograph from before dawn to after midnight and through out all the seasons. Each day the light is different, as the sun takes up its new position. In the winter, the sun sets below the Statue of Liberty, but by summertime it goes down above Central Park. It rises in a particular spot, for only one day in a year, so I have to plan from one year to the next in order to be ready to capture that unique light on a building.

New York is always changing, reinventing itself. In my books I try to capture something that has not been created before. The architecture of the city in the past decade has produced some of the best new landmarks that have ever been built. The photograph that first brought me major recognition was a picture of the Twin Towers; the last photograph that I took for this book is of the completed National September 11 Memorial designed by Michael Arad; the memorial had not been finished when I started this book. It is a powerful tribute, and a significant contribution to Manhattan. It is one of the most moving memorials and works of art that I have ever experienced. It is full of light and wonder. And so, this book is not only a look at the past but a ray of hope for the future.

Enjoy the pictures and words, go out, and explore this inspirational city!

Jake Rajs

Contents

STATUE OF LIBERTY

Liberty Island, Upper Bay of New York Harbor
Dedicated 1886
Sculptor: Frédéric Auguste Bartholdi
Architect of base: Richard Morris Hunt

The stately woman, Libertas, the Roman goddess of freedom, has stood sentinel on Bedloe's Island, at the northern end of the Upper Bay of New York Harbor, since 1886. In 1956 an Act of Congress officially renamed this small but famous bit of land Liberty Island.

The statue is such a familiar icon of New York, as well as of America's welcome to all the peoples of the world, that it might be a cliché were it not in fact so physically impressive. Few statues of such size have ever been contemplated, let alone realized. One thinks immediately of the Colossus of Rhodes, of the 3rd century BC, one of the Seven Wonders of the Ancient World. It was about 107 feet high. The Statue of Liberty, at 151 feet, was at the time of its erection by far the tallest freestanding statue that had ever been executed – as impressive, in its way, as the Empire State Building. Add in the elaborate base, and the total height is a dizzying (for a monument) 305 feet.

Liberty Enlightening the World is the formal name of the monument, which depicts an erect woman, draped in a classical gown, determinedly striding forward (her forceful stride is more evident from certain angles), holding aloft the torch of Enlightenment. She wears, over her tightly bunned hair, a distinctive, radiant crown, and in her left arm cradles a book inscribed with the date July 4, 1776. She is visible from all over New York, from the high floors of Manhattan office and apartment buildings, or from the sidewalks of the low-rise streets of Brooklyn, where, sometimes from miles inland, the walker is startled to step into a street only to discover a clear view of the statue in the harbor.

Yet, as any tourist will tell you, the best view is close-up, and even the most jaded New Yorker's pulse quickens as his harbor boat pulls near to the statue, and the full scale and majesty of the thing registers.

Some quick history: The idea for the

statue came from a French historian and political figure named Édouard René de Laboulaye (1811-83). Laboulaye, a republican, admired American democracy and was proud of the French contribution to the creation of the new nation. He conceived of the monument in 1865, but not till the Third Republic replaced the Second Empire in 1870 was Laboulaye able to get the backing of the French government, which agreed to finance the statue if America would provide the base. Laboulaye's friend, the sculptor Frédéric Auguste Bartholdi, designed the statue, which was

from 1876 to 1882 the torch-bearing arm of the statue (about the height of a four-story building), stood on display in Madison Square – the arm itself was a tourist attraction in its day. However, it was not till publisher Joseph Pulitzer, through his *New York World* newspaper, took up the cause, that the money was finally raised, and the base, designed by America's leading architect of the time, Richard Morris Hunt, completed. The dedication of the great monument to American-French friendship took place on October 28, 1886.

In 1883, as part of the fund-raising effort, New York poet Emma Lazarus agreed to write a poem related to the statue. She had just become involved in efforts to aid the Jewish victims of Russian pogroms, and this informed her poem, which was rendered in a bronze plaque affixed to the base in 1903:

Give me your tired, your poor
Your huddled masses yearning to breathe free
The wretched refuse of your teeming shore.

executed, in France, of copper over an iron frame engineered by Gustave Eiffel (whose eponymous tower in Paris would be dedicated three years after Liberty).

The base proved more difficult, as American fund-raising efforts stalled. To promote contributions to the base,

ELLIS ISLAND

Upper Bay of New York Harbor
Built 1900, restored as museum 1990
Architects: Boring & Tilton

Few place names are held in common by as many Americans as that of a small island in the Upper Bay of New York Harbor. In the late 18th and early 19th centuries the island was owned by a man named Samuel Ellis, and though little is known of him, and he had nothing to do with the eventual development of the island, his name is forever attached to it – and to the life stories of millions and millions of Americans. In 1808 the island was ceded to the United States government, which needed the land as part of a new system of harbor defenses during the maritime discord brought on by the

Napoleonic Wars. This is how the U.S. came into ownership of the island.

From the 1850s to the 1890s the government had used the old Castle Clinton, in Battery Park (where you now buy your ticket to visit Ellis Island and the Statue of Liberty), as an immigrant processing station. Most of the immigrants during those years came from Ireland and Germany. By the end of the 19th century, the demographics of immigration had changed. Chances are that if you are an American of Italian or eastern European Jewish background, your forbears came into Ellis Island. One third of all Americans can claim descent from immigrants who arrived in this country at Ellis Island.

The immigration station on Ellis Island opened in 1892. But the present, distinctive building, with its picturesque gables and four cupolaed towers, highly visible across the harbor from lower Manhattan, opened in 1900. It was designed by William Boring and Edward Tilton. One can only imagine how immigrants, as their ships pulled into the Upper Bay, passed their eyes from the Statue of Liberty to the lower Manhattan skyline to Ellis Island. On Ellis Island, immigrants were

"processed" – that is, they were checked to be sure they had some minimal means of support, that they had no contagious diseases, and so on. Though many immigrants did not make the cut, and remained on Ellis Island – the only American soil on which they would ever set foot – until a ship carried them back whence they came, the vast majority made it through without a problem. Many settled in New York, which in the early 20th century became the most demographically diverse city on earth. Many others just passed through New York en route to other cities.

Though Ellis Island served as the immigrant processing station until 1954, the character of the place changed dramatically after 1924. That was the year of the National Origins Act, when the Congress of the United States placed stringent restrictions on immigration. By the time immigration laws were liberalized, in 1965, Ellis Island was no longer in service: Immigrants now arrived by airplane, not boat, and immigration services had been set up at the airports. Thus most Latin American, Asian, and African immigrants to New York have no connection with Ellis Island.

Following more than three decades of disuse and deterioration, Boring & Tilton's main building was restored (by Beyer Blinder Belle and Finegold Alexander + Associates) and reopened as the Ellis Island National Monument and Museum. Many other buildings on the island await restoration and reuse. The main building now houses a library, as well as permanent and changing exhibitions, all with the goal of educating the public about the history of immigration.

MUSEUM OF JEWISH HERITAGE

36 Battery Place, Edmond J. Safra Plaza
Built 1997, Robert M. Morgenthau Wing 2003
Architects: Kevin Roche John Dinkeloo & Associates

Situated on the Hudson riverfront, between South Cove Park and Robert F. Wagner Jr. Park in the southern end of Battery Park City in lower Manhattan, the Museum of Jewish Heritage – A Living Memorial to the Holocaust is one of New York's most moving museums. The original part of the museum comprised the distinctive 30,000-square-foot hexagonal granite building, designed by Kevin Roche John Dinkeloo & Associates and opened in 1997. The original building is six-sided so as to evoke the Star of David as well as to commemorate the six million Jews who perished in the Holocaust. The museum, according to its own mission statement, "honors those who died by celebrating their lives – cherishing the traditions that they embraced, examining their achievements and faith, and affirming the vibrant worldwide Jewish community that is their legacy today." In other words, the museum focuses on educating visitors of all ages and backgrounds about the broad tapestry of Jewish life in the 20th and 21st centuries – before, during, and after the Holocaust.

In 2003, the 82,000-square-foot Robert M. Morgenthau Wing opened, vastly increasing the museum's space.

(Robert M. Morgenthau, born 1919, served as District Attorney for New York County from 1975 to 2009.) The new wing includes the 4,150-square-foot outdoor "Garden of Stones" by the British environmental artist Andy Goldsworthy. The garden comprises eighteen hollowed-out boulders that range from three to thirteen tons. Eighteen is the numerical value of the Hebrew word chai – "life." From each boulder grows a dwarf oak sapling. Goldsworthy said he got the idea for the work when he was staying in a midtown hotel. He looked out his window and saw that a tree had taken root in the side of a building across the way. To the artist that tree symbolized the tenaciousness of life.

In addition to changing exhibitions, the museum features a Core Exhibition divided into three sections: Jewish Life a Century Ago, The War Against the Jews, and Jewish Renewal, each on its own floor. The museum could not be more felicitously sited, as it looks out upon New York Harbor with a clear vista of the Statue of Liberty and Ellis Island. The museum is a stirring testament to the Jewish experience in the 20th and 21st centuries, and to the central role of New York in the history of the Jewish migrations during that time.

THE WINTER GARDEN

Enter from Vesey Street west of West Street
Built 1985-88, reconstructed 2002
Architects: Cesar Pelli & Associates, Diana Balmori, landscape architect

The Winter Garden was New York's grandest public space in a generation when it opened in 1988. Roughly of the dimensions of the Main Concourse of Grand Central Terminal, the giant greenhouse, designed by Cesar Pelli and Diana Balmori, faces the majestic Hudson River, visible through a dramatic high glass wall across an outdoor waterfront plaza adorned with artworks by Scott Burton and Siah Armajani.

The Winter Garden is very 1980s in a number of ways. That decade saw a return among architects to the use of masonry revetments, though the soaring cost of fine stone led builders to apply only paper-thin veneers of stone. Another trend of the time was the incorporation into lobbies and atriums of exotic vegetation. Here we have sixteen 40-foot-high *Washingtonia robusta* palm trees, an unexpected sight in Manhattan.

This grand, light-filled space is at the pivot of, and provides access to, a group of office buildings known as Brookfield Place, originally comprising four office buildings completed between 1985 and 1987 and containing more than seven million square feet of floor area. The four towers currently provide homes to American Express, Dow Jones & Co., Merrill Lynch, Deloitte & Touche, Cadwalader, Wickersham & Taft, and other "blue chip" firms. These office buildings in their turn are part of a much larger complex of apartment buildings and public parks called Battery Park City, a whole new waterfront neighborhood that began to take shape around 1980.

Originally, a 400-foot-long aerial bridge over West Street connected the Winter Garden to the World Trade Center. On September 11, 2001, the bridge was destroyed, and the Winter Garden was smashed to bits, its thousands of glass panes shattered, and its grand marble staircase, which had led to the aerial bridge, crushed to rubble. The rapid reconstruction of the Winter Garden within one year of the terrible day was a sign of hope for all New Yorkers. President George W. Bush attended the formal reopening of the Winter Garden on September 17, 2002.

The Winter Garden now is the anchor to a new luxury retail area and food court.

ONE WORLD TRADE CENTER

Bounded by Liberty, West, Vesey, and Church Streets
World Trade Center dedicated 1973, destroyed 2001
One World Trade Center completed 2014
Architects of first World Trade Center: Minoru Yamasaki and Emery Roth & Sons
Architects of One World Trade Center: Skidmore, Owings & Merrill

The World Trade Center was dedicated in 1973. On the site (which until recently most people called "Ground Zero", though many New Yorkers preferred to call it the "World Trade Center site"), bounded by Liberty Street on the south, West Street on the west, Vesey Street on the north, and Church Street on the east, stood six buildings, Nos. 1-6 World Trade Center. Nos. 1 and 2 were the "twin towers." Two World Trade Center ("Tower 2" as it came to be known) stood along Liberty Street at the northeast corner of the line of Greenwich Street. (Four blocks of the north-south Greenwich Street were demapped when the World Trade Center superblock was created in the 1960s.) One World Trade Center stood just to the north, along West Street roughly on the line of Dey Street. Nos. 4 and 5 stood on Church Street between Liberty and Vesey Streets (No. 5 directly across the street from the ancient churchyard of St. Paul's Chapel), and No. 6 was at the southeast corner of West and Vesey Streets. Each of these buildings was designed by the Seattle-

based Japanese-American architect Minoru Yamasaki with the prolific Manhattan office design firm of Emery Roth & Sons. No. 3, originally the Vista International Hotel (later the Marriott World Trade Center), at the northeast corner of West and Liberty, was designed by Skidmore, Owings & Merrill.

Greenwich Street, the line of which neatly bisects the site into eastern and western halves, is the original shoreline in this part of Manhattan. That means that everything to the west of Greenwich is landfill. Out to West Street most of the landfill was done in the 18th and 19th centuries. Beyond West Street, where Battery Park City now extends from Battery Place to Chambers Street, the landfill was done in the 1960s. About a quarter of that landfill came from excavations for the World Trade Center, which means that Battery Park City is built on landfill that came in part from earlier landfill!

The World Trade Center was built by the Port Authority of New York and New Jersey, which at first seems odd. Why would the bi-state super-governmental public authority, whose mandate extended solely to the coordination of port and transportation infrastructure and operations involving both states, be the developer of a mega-complex of business buildings in lower Manhattan? The answer is that before the World Trade Center, a portion of its land was occupied by an earlier pair of twin towers, the Hudson Terminal Buildings. These were owned by the Hudson & Manhattan Railroad, which operated a busy train station below the two large office buildings. The Hudson & Manhattan was the main commuter line serving New Jersey residents who

worked in Manhattan. When the line faced bankruptcy, the Port Authority stepped in to prop it up, and in so doing came into proprietorship of several acres of lower Manhattan land. (The Port Authority renamed the railroad to Port Authority Trans-Hudson, or PATH.)

Minoru Yamasaki was at first an acclaimed choice to be the designer of the complex. His fame in the 1960s rested principally on his work in Saudi Arabia, where he skillfully wove Islamic motifs into his otherwise thoroughly modern designs. While his twin towers became iconic New York buildings, it's also true that some New Yorkers, including most architecture critics, disliked them, for their distorting scale, the aridity of the public spaces, and the destruction of a lively old neighborhood. It's also true that the center came on the market at a bad time, and was tenanted only by siphoning government offices from other lower Manhattan buildings.

Still, no one was left other than emotionally devastated by what occurred on September 11, 2001, when two passenger jetliners that had been hijacked by Islamic militants were flown deliberately into the two towers. Later in the day the towers collapsed in spectacular fashion, imploding or "pancaking" (as opposed to tipping over), raising a storm of dust and debris that left lower Manhattan under a months-long gray blanket. However, the manner of implosion meant that remarkably little damage was done outside the center footprint. One might have expected diminutive old St. Paul's to have been pulverized; it was barely scratched. Nearly three thousand people died on the day of greatest infamy in the history of New York.

Today, a new World Trade Center complex is nearing completion on the site. The new 1,776-foot-high One World Trade Center (designed by David Childs of Skidmore, Owings & Merrill though evolved from a competition-winning design by Studio Daniel Libeskind that had to be extensively reworked in response to security concerns), Fumihiko Maki's Four World Trade Center, and The National September 11 Memorial and Museum, by Michael Arad and Peter Walker, are complete.

And, eventually, two other towers will rise, as well as a highly anticipated new PATH station by the exciting Spanish architect-engineer Santiago Calatrava.

As the construction fences continue to come down and with the Memorial Plaza now providing pedestrian access to the towers, transit hub, and surrounding streets, the area formally known as Ground Zero will be far more than just a new business and commercial complex. It will forever be a site of pilgrimage and remembrance.

FEDERAL HALL NATIONAL MEMORIAL

(originally U.S. Custom House)
26 Wall Street, opposite Broad Street
Built 1833-42
Architects: Ithiel Town and Alexander Jackson Davis

This was built as the United States Custom House between 1833 and 1842, the long duration indicating that construction was stalled by the Panic of 1837. The building replaced the old Federal Hall where George Washington took his oath of office as first president of the United States of America. The April 30, 1789, event is commemorated by a superb statue, dedicated in 1883 (the centennial of the British evacuation from New York), of Washington by John Quincy Adams Ward.

The present building later became the U.S. Subtreasury and then, in 1939, a national historic site, and, in 1955, a national memorial. It is now, in effect, a memorial to the previous building on the site, as well as to George Washington and the founding of the republic. However, it is in itself one of the finest buildings in the city. The Greek Revival in architecture was stimulated in part by the discoveries of 18th-century archaeologists, and also by an early

19th-century Romantic Movement that idolized past civilizations and indulged a melancholy cult of ruins. Temple-front buildings, often patterned after the 5th-century BC Parthenon, appeared in Europe and America. In the U.S., the cult of Greek architecture merged with the national conviction that Americans were the heirs of the Athenian democratic tradition. So thoroughly did "Grecian" architecture (as it was called) sweep the nation that the columned, temple-front building seemed as American as apple pie and baseball.

But note something about Federal Hall National Memorial: It is topped off by a pitched roof, with the gable end facing Wall Street. The gable is defined as a "pediment" by its raking cornices. In ancient Greece, this triangular space would have been a picture frame, filled with elaborate, polychrome figure sculpture. However, here, as in all the buildings of the American Greek Revival, those picture frames were left empty. One reason may be that the architects were less interested in how the Greeks actually built than in the ruins of Greek buildings, in which all the delicate decoration had worn away. The blank pediments were meant to evoke a melancholy sentiment, a ruefulness that ran in a strong current through antebellum American culture. But there is another reason for the absence of elaborate carving: When

Federal Hall National Memorial was built, New York possessed few skilled carvers. Subsequent immigration would flood the city with skilled craftsmen of all kinds. Look across Broad Street to the New York Stock Exchange (1903, George B. Post, architect). By the time it was built, there were more skilled Italian carvers in America than there were in Italy. The pediment there is crammed with elaborate figures.

Federal Hall National Memorial was constructed of marble from Westchester County, laid in great blocks without mortar – just as the ancient Greeks had built. Go inside to see the splendid rotunda, with most of its 1840s details intact. It is one of the great spaces of New York. You feel transported to the America of Andrew Jackson.

WALL STREET, NEW YORK STOCK EXCHANGE & TRINITY CHURCH

Broad Street at Wall Street
Built 1901-03
Architect: George B. Post

The largest stock exchange in the world (measured by the value of the companies traded) had humble origins. Shortly after the Revolution, New York auctioneers began to sell consignments of government paper to the highest bidder. Auctions took place in the Merchants Coffee House at Wall and Water Streets, and dealers and brokers would gather outside to swap stocks. A preferred spot for such trading was on Wall Street between Hanover and Pearl Streets, under a buttonwood (or sycamore) tree. In early 1792 a panic hit the securities market, which had been heavily manipulated by a group of investors led by William Duer, and the city was momentarily brought to its knees before the deft interventions of Treasury Secretary Alexander Hamilton prevented a bad situation from getting worse. That's when dealers and brokers signed the so-

called "Buttonwood Agreement", which eliminated the auctioneers (thus cutting down on the manipulation of securities prices) and fixing brokers' commissions. Oh, and they decided to move indoors: It was more seemly.

In 1817 the brokers' group named itself the New York Stock & Exchange Board, and in 1863 simplified the name to the present New York Stock Exchange. From 1842 to 1854 the Exchange had operated out of 55 Wall Street, a beautiful building still standing (although its original dome was replaced at the beginning of the 20th century with the present top story). In 1865 the exchange built a new building at its present location on Broad Street, just south of Wall Street. After the Civil War the Exchange grew rapidly, together with the American economy. In this era of westward expansion and industrial development, when the telegraph, telephone, and railroad conquered space and time, New York, led by its Exchange, emerged not only as America's greatest financial center, but as one of the most important financial centers in the world.

Between 1901 and 1903 the old Exchange building was demolished and the present building, designed by George B. Post, was built. At the beginning of the new century, New York stood poised to claim its place among the greatest cities on earth, the true peer of London and Paris. This swagger is evident in the architecture of Post's Exchange building. It is instructive to compare the Exchange with Federal Hall National Memorial across Wall Street. The latter building, erected between 1833 and 1842, represents a simpler America, a nation largely without imperial ambitions. The Greek Revival architecture is simple, chaste, rugged, and even a bit melancholy. Though the building is marble, it is the dingy-hued marble of Westchester County, New York. The Exchange, by contrast, is anything but chaste: The Vermont marble gleams, the florid Corinthian order contrasts with the Doric of Federal Hall National Memorial. Most striking of all is how the Exchange's front gable, articulated as a pediment with raking (slanting) cornices, is filled with figure sculpture, in stark contrast to the earlier Federal Hall National Memorial. Such pediments are meant to be picture frames. By 1900, mass immigration had brought the world's best carvers to New York. And in the richest city in the world, a building without sculptural embellishment was unthinkable.

Post's building has witnessed and endured many monumental events and cataclysms: the Panic of 1907, World War I (after which New York became the world's most important financial center), the Crash of 1929 and the Great Depression, World War II (after which New York led the world in every conceivable measurable criterion of greatness), the crash of 1987, the global economic calamity of 2008, and more. Through it all, the building has remained as great a symbol of New York as any structure in the city.

SOUTH STREET SEAPORT

Bounded by John, Front, Beekman, and South Streets
Older buildings built early 19th century, newer buildings 1980s
Principal architect of the redevelopment:
Benjamin Thompson & Associates

New York's reason for being is its harbor. It is one of the great natural harbors – indeed one of the great natural wonders – of the world. The dumbbell-shaped harbor has a Lower Bay that yields, via a narrow channel between Long Island and Staten Island, to an Upper Bay, known as a "protected" harbor. In the days of wooden sailing ships, the East River docks along South Street provided further protection; the Hudson was just too open and wind-tossed. Later, when ships were bigger, made of steel, and powered by steam, the Hudson docks superseded the East River ones. However, back in the classic days of sailing across the oceans, South Street ruled and was the source of the city's earliest fortunes.

South Street saw many innovations. The Black Ball Line operated from the foot of Peck Slip. In 1818 it inaugurated the first regularly scheduled service across the Atlantic. Before that, ships sailed only when their holds were full. But Black Ball changed all that; the service came to be known as "packet shipping" (after the mail packets Black Ball was contracted to carry), and it was one of the profound innovations that made New York's the most successful seaport in the nation.

It was from South Street that the great clippers of the 1840s and 1850s were launched. These sleek, high-masted sailing ships, manufactured in the great shipyards farther up the East River, were designed by master naval architects for New York merchants engaged in the lucrative trade with China. One after another, the clipper ships set speed records. Great crowds came to South Street to witness the launches of the beautiful ships, and their records riveted the public like great sporting events.

The rise of steam meant the decline of South Street. After the Civil War, South Street's importance waned until it took on a forlorn character. The old seaport buildings, some dating back to the 18th century and once associated with some of the greatest mercantile fortunes in America, decayed until, inevitably, many were cleared away for the construction of high-rise office buildings. The major exception was the Fulton Fish Market, the city's wholesale fish market. Yet its early morning bustle – not unlike that on the trading floor of the New York Stock Exchange – lasted only until 2005 when, after 183 years on the site, the market was shifted to Hunt's Point in the Bronx.

The South Street Seaport festival marketplace, with new and restored buildings housing food stalls, bars, and boutiques, as well as an enhanced Seaport Museum, opened in 1983. Architecturally, the most arresting part of the new development was the refurbishment of old Schermerhorn

Row, a block of early 19th-century countinghouses and warehouses along Fulton Street between Front Street and South Street.

As a result of damage from Hurricane Sandy parts of South Street Seaport are being redeveloped to include a new entertainment complex which will be completed in 2016 and include a 4,000 seat amphitheater.

SKYSCRAPER MUSEUM

39 Battery Place (in the Ritz Carlton in Battery Park City)
Built 2004
Architects: Skidmore, Owings & Merrill

New York once had an appearance unique among all the cities of the world. It was the world's first high-rise city. Visitors in the early 20th century were sometimes appalled, but never less than amazed, by what they saw.

Most people today would not recognize the earliest skyscrapers as such. The Equitable Building of 1868-70, on Broadway and Cedar Street, was only seven stories high, but rose to 130 feet, and had a passenger elevator. The elevator was key: Because of it, upper floors rented for the same money as lower floors. Since the whole point of a skyscraper was to multiply the value of a plot of land, the financial model introduced by the Equitable Building makes it, in the view of many historians, the first skyscraper.

Further developments, including the use of iron and steel framing and advances in fireproofing and wind-bracing technology, allowed buildings to rise ever higher. Manhattan is notable as a place with many buildings that once boasted of being the tallest in the world: the Park Row Building (1899), the Metropolitan Life Insurance Company Tower (1909), the Woolworth Building (1913), 40 Wall Street (1929), the Chrysler Building (1930), and the Empire State Building (1931). The twin towers of the World Trade Center (opened 1973) briefly held the title. Today, the Empire State Building, the tallest in New York, is the 12th tallest building in the world; the Burj Khalifa, in Dubai, is more than twice as high.

It is only fitting that in New York of all cities there should be a Skyscraper Museum. Founded in 1996 by the architectural historian Carol Willis, for its first few years the museum lacked a permanent home. But in 2004 the Skyscraper Museum moved into space donated by Millennium Partners in a new 38-story condominium and hotel tower at the southern end of Battery Park City. What's more, Skidmore, Owings & Merrill, led by partner Roger Duffy, designed for the museum a dramatic space, appropriately strong in vertical accents and canyon-like passageways that call to mind the skyscraper city outside the museum's doors. There is space for both a permanent core exhibit (Skyscraper/City) and for changing exhibits. The British historian Paul Johnson once wrote that the groves of skyscrapers in American cities represent "perhaps the greatest achievement of twentieth-century art." And New York has a great museum to celebrate the phenomenon.

BROOKLYN BRIDGE

Enter the pedestrian walkway at Centre Street and Park Row
Built 1870-83
Architects: John Augustus Roebling and Washington Augustus Roebling

The Brooklyn Bridge opened in the centennial year of the end of the American Revolution, fittingly capping a century in which America had put the world on notice that, when it came to astonishing feats of technical ingenuity, the new nation was second to no other nation on earth. And New York contributed more than its fair share of these feats, beginning with the Erie Canal, which opened in 1825. That was a larger public-works project than had ever been undertaken in Europe. Then came the city's Croton water system, and Central Park; and then the Brooklyn Bridge, by far the longest suspension bridge that had ever been constructed anywhere in the world.

The measurement for a suspension bridge is its "main span" between the towers from which the cables that hold

the roadway aloft are suspended. The main span of the Brooklyn Bridge is 1,595.5 feet. It surpassed its nearest rival, the 1,057-foot Cincinnati-Covington Bridge (completed in 1866), by more than 50 percent.

One of the things that made America so accomplished at such a young age is that the nation drew upon the talents of people from all over the world. Both the Cincinnati and Brooklyn Bridges were designed by the same man, a German, named John Augustus Roebling. (The Cincinnati-Covington Bridge has since been renamed the John A. Roebling Bridge.) Roebling was a polymath. In addition to being such a gifted engineer, he had been a favored pupil of the great German philosopher Hegel. Roebling came to America to found a utopian community in Pennsylvania; the community failed, but Roebling built a business manufacturing his patented wire rope, which was far stronger than cloth rope and found wide use in canal and bridge projects. He first proposed that New York build an East River bridge when in 1852 he got stuck on an ice-bound ferry on the river. But not until 1865 did the necessary approvals and financing come through, and not until 1870 did construction commence.

It was an epic undertaking. The Brooklyn tower was completed in 1875, the Manhattan in 1876. There are four steel-wire cables, each containing 3,515

miles of wire. Attached to the cables are 208 suspenders, giving to the bridge its exquisite web-like appearance. The towers were built atop the largest pneumatic caissons ever constructed. These were large watertight chambers from which workers excavated into the river bed in search of bedrock; at the end the chambers were filled with concrete. The bodily effects of the pressure inside the caissons were poorly understood, and workers were afflicted with "caisson disease," or decompression sickness. Fifteen workers died from decompression

sickness. Overall, 27 men died in the construction of the bridge.

It opened on May 24, 1883, when President Chester A. Arthur walked across the bridge while a band played "Hail to the Chief."

But John Roebling had not seen it built. He had died in 1869 when he contracted tetanus after his foot got smashed in a freak ferryboat accident. His brilliant, equally polymathic, and often melancholy son, Washington Augustus Roebling, took over the project. However, invalided by caisson

disease, he was forced to oversee construction from his house on Brooklyn Heights, through a telescope. The on-the-job supervisor was Washington's remarkable wife, Emily Warren Roebling, now rightly regarded as the third designer of the Brooklyn Bridge. When President Arthur walked from the Manhattan to the Brooklyn end of the bridge on that spring day in 1883, he was greeted by Brooklyn Mayor Seth Low, and by Emily Roebling.

It lost its world's-longest title in 1903 when another New York bridge, the Williamsburg Bridge, nosed it out. Then in 1931 New York set a new record with the 3,500-foot George Washington Bridge. New York's longest today, and 8th longest in the world, is the Verrazano-Narrows Bridge, at 4,260 feet long (or 2664.5 feet longer than the Brooklyn Bridge). Today, Brooklyn Bridge is only the 77th longest suspension bridge in the world and several longer bridges are already under construction. But no bridge in its time startled the world as did the Brooklyn; and none is as beautiful, or as exciting to walk across.

AFRICAN BURIAL GROUND

Visitor Center and Memorial, Duane Street between Broadway and Elk Street (African Burial Ground Way)
Memorial dedicated 2007
Memorial by Rodney Leon with Nicole Hollant-Denis

Slavery was not confined to the American South. Not only was slavery legal in New York until 1827, but slave ownership rates were high, and the African slave trade was an early linchpin of the city economy. Slave labor was employed in many of the city's early public-works projects, such as the building of the Post Road to Boston, and the draining of the Collect Pond, or fresh water lake, in lower Manhattan.

It is very important to the memory of New York slaves that there be a fitting monument to the monstrous history that led defenseless Africans into forced labor halfway across the world. New York's monument to this inglorious past is the African Burial Ground National Monument.

Up to the early 19th century, well-to-do white New Yorkers, when they died, were buried in the churchyards, such as the ones every visitor to New York sees at Trinity Church and St. Paul's Chapel, both on lower Broadway. Poor white New Yorkers were buried in potter's fields – there was one under the present Washington Square. But black New Yorkers, slaves and free blacks alike, had their own burial ground.

The five-acre African Burial Ground was located just to the north of the present City Hall. It is believed that between 10,000 and 20,000 black men, women, and children were interred there between 1712 and 1794. As is the fate of so many urban graveyards, the African Burial Ground was paved over and built upon. It was also largely forgotten. This all changed in 1991 with the beginning of construction of the Ted Weiss Federal Building on Broadway between Reade and Duane Streets.

When remains were found during excavations for the Federal Building, construction was halted. Archaeologists unearthed bodies and artifacts. Eventually a team from Washington, D.C.'s Howard University was put in charge of examining and then respectfully reinterring the

remains. The Federal Building (designed by Hellmuth Obata & Kassabaum) was redesigned so that a portion of the Burial Ground, at the southwest corner of Duane Street and Elk Street (since renamed African Burial Ground Way), would remain as an open space containing a memorial. Much of the lobby of the new Federal Building was given to an educational and commemorative exhibit on the Burial Ground.

The Burial Ground site was declared a National Historic Landmark in 1993. In 2006, it was elevated to National Monument status, one of only 101 sites in the country to be so honored. (The only others in New York City include Castle Clinton, Governors Island, and the Statue of Liberty.)

The outdoor memorial was created by Rodney Leon with Nicole Hollant-Denis of Brooklyn's AARRIS Architects. It was dedicated on October 5, 2007. A great granite wedge bearing texts points into a large bowl inscribed with a map of the Atlantic Ocean, representing the Middle Passage that brought the enslaved from West Africa to North America. It is a thematically dense work that speaks:

For all those who were lost
For all those who were stolen
For all those who were left behind
For all those who are not forgotten

Completed in 2010, the visitor center in the lobby of the Federal Building, includes educational materials and a life-size tableau of a funeral in the Burial Ground. There is also a small theater and a shop.

WOOLWORTH BUILDING

Broadway between Barclay Street and Park Place
Built 1910-13
Architect: Cass Gilbert

"The Cathedral of Commerce" is what America's most famous early 20th-century preacher, the Reverend Samuel Parkes Cadman, called the Woolworth Building when it was erected. The builder was Frank Winfield Woolworth, the five-and-dime king whose retail empire began in Lancaster, Pennsylvania, in 1879 and by 1910 spanned the globe. He told his architect, Cass Gilbert, that he wanted something like London's Houses of Parliament, and Gilbert obliged with a soaring tower covered in lacy Gothic ornamentation executed in gleaming white terra-cotta. At 57 stories, the Woolworth Building overtook the Metropolitan Life Insurance Company Tower as the world's tallest building, and held the title for sixteen years, or until 40 Wall Street was completed. In an era of growing national self-confidence, the Woolworth Building was a great symbol of American pride. Indeed, on the evening of the day the building officially opened for business, President Woodrow Wilson flipped a switch in the White House and turned on all the Woolworth Building's electric lights.

The lobby is as impressive as the exterior, with stunning mosaics, murals, and stained glass reflecting the extraordinary standard of crafts-manship of the time. The Woolworth company was so proud of the lobby that it encouraged people to visit, and the lobby guards were always extremely welcoming to passersby who wished to stop in and gawk. Since Woolworth's demise and 1998 sale of the building, new owners have taken a different tack: The beautiful lobby now is viewed as a perquisite of building tenancy, and is strictly off-limits to the public.

Long the dominant skyline building in the neighborhood of City Hall Park, the Woolworth was for thirty years overshadowed by the nearby twin towers of the World Trade Center. How strange it was following September 11, 2001, to see the Woolworth again com-mand the sky.

8 SPRUCE STREET

Between Nassau and William Streets
Built 2006-11
Architect: Frank Gehry

In 2011 an apartment block, 8 Spruce Street, right on the other side of City Hall Park between Nassau and William Streets, overtopped the Woolworth Building by 75 feet (867 feet to 792 feet). The 76-story 8 Spruce Street is the first super-tall building (currently ranked 128th tallest in the world, but slipping fast, while the Woolworth has fallen out of the top 200) designed by the distinguished Canadian-born architect Frank Gehry, famed for his Guggenheim Museum in Bilbao, Spain, and his Walt Disney Concert Hall in Los Angeles. The distinctive tower (which incorporates a public school and a hospital annex) has a unique facade resembling long bolts of fabric fluttering in the breeze.

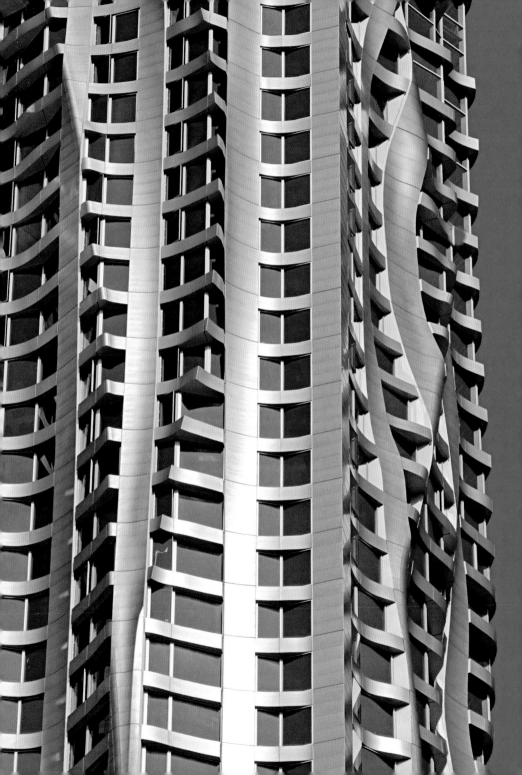

CHINATOWN

Roughly bounded by Grand and Essex Streets, Broadway, and the Brooklyn Bridge

The first Chinese in New York came in the late 18th and early 19th centuries when New York had become a major port in the China trade. But these Chinese merchants and sailors were transients, and a real Chinese community did not form in New York until the completion of the trans-continental railroad (which had provided many jobs for Chinese immigrants in the western United States) and growing anti-Chinese sentiment in the West pushed many Chinese eastward. The Chinese Exclusion Act of 1882 placed a severe restriction on the numbers of Chinese in the country, and New York's Chinatown was a largely male preserve. Restrictions eased somewhat during World War II when China and the U.S. were allies. But it was the immigration reform legislation passed by Congress in 1965 that led to the vast increase in Chinese – and other Asian – New Yorkers.

Fixing the boundaries of Manhattan's Chinatown is extremely difficult. Chinatown has sprawled to encompass most of the historically Jewish Lower East Side (the Garden Cafeteria, on East Broadway, where the writers of the Yiddish-language *Jewish Daily Forward* gathered over matzah ball soup, is now a restaurant called Wing Shoon, known for its dim sum), Little Italy, and the area of the legendary Five Points slum.

On Chatham Square, in some ways the heart of Chinatown, is the memorial to Benjamin Ralph Kimlau. A Chinese-American who became a U.S. Army Air Forces bomber pilot in World War II, he was killed in action in 1944. The memorial is notable for its inclusion of calligraphy by Yu Youren (1879-1964), considered China's greatest modern master of the art of calligraphy. Another notable nearby monument is the bronze statue of Confucius, the

great Chinese philosopher of the 6th century BC, by the Taiwanese sculptor Liu Shih; it dates from 1977.

But one does not go to Chinatown seeking monuments so much as the frenetic life of the tenement-packed streets. Food stores spill produce and fish onto the sidewalks, cornucopia-like, while restaurants and food counters occupy both grand premises, the size of banquet halls, and broom-closet-size spaces virtually hidden down a flight of stairs. Store signs, advertisements, and even cash machines in bank branches are in Mandarin and Cantonese. No other part of Manhattan continues to prove the adage that for the cost of a subway fare a New Yorker can travel to the other side of the world.

SOHO CAST IRON DISTRICT

Bounded by Houston Street on the north, Canal Street on the south,
West Broadway on the west, and Crosby Street on the east
Haughwout Building Broadway and Broome Street
Built 1857
Architect: J.P. Gaynor

SoHo is an acronym for SOuth of HOuston Street. In the 1820s this was *the* fashionable residential neighborhood. Remnants of all periods of a neighborhood's history can still be found by the alert explorer. On the west side of Greene Street, just south of Houston Street, stands a dilapidated Federal-style red-brick row house (139 Greene Street), built in 1825. The owners of this house moved out in 1860, and the house was converted into a brothel. Brothels existed in great numbers in these streets, making this the city's "red light district." But part of the area was also, in the 1850s and 1860s, the city's most fashionable shopping district.

One building from this era that no visitor to SoHo should miss is the former E.V. Haughwout (pronounced How-it) Store. This was among the first of the area's soon to be many cast-iron-fronted commercial buildings. Builders liked using iron cast from molds for the ease with which elaborate ornamental patterns could be replicated, and because cast iron allowed for larger window openings.

From the 1870s to the 1960s, this was an industrial neighborhood. Most of the old houses and hotels and stores were replaced by garment factories and textile warehouses. After World War II artists began moving into the old industrial buildings.

It's a truism of New York life that where the artists go, others follow. Unfortunately, the others typically have far more money than the artists, and the money drives up the cost of living. Today SoHo is one of the most expensive urban residential neighborhoods in America.

When these buildings were imperiled by an ultimately thwarted 1960s plan to strap an expressway across lower Manhattan, an architectural historian named Margot Gayle led volunteers in an effort to catalogue the many cast-iron buildings. Since many had been designed to look like they were made of stone, and it was hard to tell which were cast iron and which were stone, the cataloguers adopted the expedient of placing magnets to the buildings' surfaces. Try it, and marvel at the beauty of Victorian ironwork.

LOWER EAST SIDE: TENEMENT MUSEUM, ELDRIDGE STREET SYNAGOGUE, KATZ'S DELICATESSEN

The Lower East Side of Manhattan is today partly swallowed up by Chinatown, which has grown explosively in recent decades, and partly one of the city's trendiest neighborhoods in which to live and play.

To anyone who lived on the Lower East Side a century ago, the idea that it would ever be a trendy place to live and play – a place of Michelin-starred restaurants, raucous bars for the post-college crowd, and expensive condominiums designed by world-famous architects – would have been laughable.

Nothing tells the story of the old East Side as does the Lower East Side Tenement Museum at 97 Orchard Street, between Delancey and Broome Streets. As mass immigration swelled the population of the very poor in New York in the 1840s and 1850s, a new building type arose: the purpose-built, multiple-family dwelling we call the tenement. At first, few laws existed to ensure a minimum level of amenities in such buildings. Builders of tenement housing typically sought to pack as many units as they could on the standard 20-foot-by-100-foot New York building lot. Streets of tenements were so densely built that no light or air from outside could penetrate into most of the rooms in the building. And builders also dispensed with unnecessary luxuries – like toilets! Crowding and sanitary conditions were appalling. Not until the Tenement House Act of 1879 and, especially, the Tenement

House Act of 1901 were truly meaningful steps taken to combat the scourge of tenement life in New York. The tenement building at 97 Orchard Street dates from 1863, before these laws were passed. When 97 Orchard was built, the neighborhood was part of Kleindeutschland, or "Little Germany." By the end of the 19th century, the Germans had moved on, and eastern European Jews had moved in. Around 1900, the block bounded by Orchard, Delancey, Broome, and Allen Streets was populated at the density equivalent of about 600,000 people per square mile; the East Side as a whole came in around 300,000; Manhattan as a whole about 90,000. This was the most crowded block in the most crowded neighborhood in the most crowded city in America. However, the immigration restrictions put in place by the federal government beginning in 1924, halted the yearly flood of newcomers who replaced those who moved out, and the East Side rapidly depopulated. For more than half a century, 97 Orchard Street actually stood empty.

In 1988 Ruth Abram and Anita Jacobson began the process of converting 97 Orchard into America's first museum of tenement history, with apartments restored to show what life was like for the different immigrant groups that occupied the building from 1863 to its shuttering in 1935.

More of the old Jewish East Side can be seen a few blocks to the south, at the

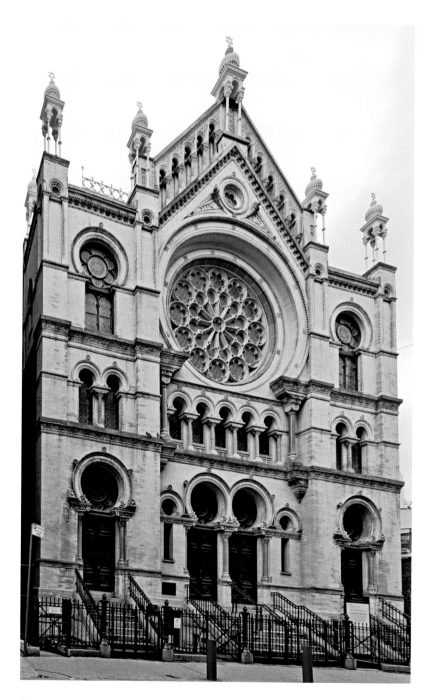

Eldridge Street Synagogue, on Eldridge Street between Canal and Division Streets. Built in 1887, this was the first New York synagogue built by eastern European Jews, and one of the grandest synagogues in the city. For half a century the congregation numbered in the thousands. But the depopulation of the neighborhood took its toll, and just as 97 Orchard was shuttered, so, from 1955 to 1980, was the synagogue's main sanctuary. All but forgotten, the synagogue was rediscovered by New York historian and tour guide Gerard R. Wolfe, who in 1971 was the first person in many years to peer inside the magnificent sanctuary. "I cannot forget," Wolfe wrote, "how my hair stood up and goose pimples arose on my back." Thus began the decades-long project of restoration (under the direction of Roberta Brandes Gratz) that has resulted in the opening of the Museum at Eldridge Street in 2007.

No visit to the Jewish East Side would be complete without food. Katz's Delicatessen, on Houston and Ludlow Streets, is as historic a Jewish eatery as there is in New York. Katz's opened in 1888, just as Jewish immigration into New York had gone from wave to tsunami. It is the place to go for pastrami and hot dogs, and is a popular location for movies, most famously *When Harry Met Sally* (1989) with Meg Ryan and Billy Crystal.

THE NEW MUSEUM OF CONTEMPORARY ART

235 Bowery at Stanton Street
Built 2007
Architects: SANAA (Kazuyo Sejima and Ryue Nishizawa)

The Bowery in the 19th century was the Broadway of working-class New York, a thronged thoroughfare of theaters and bars where the b'hoys and g'hals paraded in their flamboyant costumes. Later, the Bowery became New York's street of lost souls, a place of flophouses, and of winos sprawled on the pavements. It was at the same time where the wholesale dealers in restaurant equipment were located. (Want to open a restaurant? Many of the dealers – in restaurant ranges, diner booths, deli slicing machines, cash registers – still ply their trade on the Bowery.)

The Bowery has been many things.
But trendy? Artistic?

Well, today it is. In fact, artists have been living or working on and near the Bowery for many years. Alex Katz, Hans Haacke, Elizabeth Murray, Cy Twombly, Robert Frank, Brice Marden, Kenneth Noland, Mark Rothko, Vito Acconci, Roy Lichtenstein, Sarah Charlesworth, Dorothea Rockburne, Eva Hesse, and Maya Lin are just some of the well-known artists who have kept studios or homes on or just off the Bowery.

The New Museum of Contemporary Art was founded by Whitney Museum of American Art curator Marcia Tucker in 1977. In 1983 the Museum moved into a building on Broadway between Houston and Prince Streets in SoHo. In 2002 the New Museum, now under the direction of another former Whitney curator, Lisa Phillips, announced that it was going to build a new facility on the site of a parking lot at 235 Bowery. The new building opened on December 1, 2007.

The design by the Japanese architects Kazuyo Sejima and Ryue Nishizawa may be the most eye-catching thing on the Bowery. It is in the form of six seemingly precariously stacked boxes that look as though they may tumble down, sheathed in gray metal covered in a wire mesh that adds texture to the facades. Because the volumes are not perfectly aligned one atop the other, there is the opportunity for each floor of the museum to have a skylight. The architects' carefully thought-out minimalism has won plaudits from many critics, who also note that the radical design does not seem out of place on its rough-and-tumble thoroughfare.

The New Museum was conceived as an institution that would operate in an area halfway between the city's experimental art spaces and the established museums. As such it has presented countless important exhibitions of such artists as Keith Haring, Jeff Koons, Jenny Holzer, Louise Bourgeois, Martin Puryear, David Wojnarowicz, and many others.

Two doors to the south of the New Museum is the Bowery Mission, founded in 1879 and in its present building since 1909. The Mission, which ministers to the destitute, represents the Bowery of a century ago; the New Museum, the Bowery of today. At least for now, they coexist on one of the most interesting thoroughfares in Manhattan.

COOPER UNION

8th Street between Cooper Square and Third Avenue
Built 1853-59
Architect: Frederick A. Peterson

Peter Cooper (1791-1883) was born in the humblest of circumstances and through extraordinary hard work and a native intelligence that had not had the benefit of formal schooling made of himself one of the great tycoons of America. But he never took without giving back, and in the 1850s formed Cooper Union as an institution of higher learning that would offer its courses free of charge, that would not discriminate on the basis of race or sex, and that would offer classes and lectures at hours convenient to common laborers.

Frederick A. Peterson's building is a somber affair, coated in the brown sandstone that was taking over New York, in the Germanic style known as Rundbogenstil ("round-arched style"). The building appeared a tad less ponderous before its original graceful roofline was destroyed in the 1880s by the addition of a story.

On February 27, 1860, presidential candidate Abraham Lincoln came to deliver a speech in the Great Hall of Cooper Union. It is said to have won him the Republican nomination and, shortly thereafter, the presidency.

For many years the ground floor housed the Museum for the Arts of Decoration; in 1976 it moved from here to the former Andrew Carnegie mansion on Fifth Avenue and 91st Street and was renamed the Cooper-Hewitt Museum, a branch of the Smithsonian Institution. The space in the old building was then transformed into the school's library, designed by John Hejduk, for many years a highly influential teacher of architecture at Cooper Union. Today Cooper Union is known as a school of art, architecture, and engineering. The prestigious institution is still tuition-free, the shining legacy of one of the greatest of all New Yorkers.

On the block to south stands a highly distinctive addition to the Cooper Union campus. Designed by Pritzker Prize-winning California architect Thom Mayne, 41 Cooper Square, completed in 2009, is a large metallic cube with a great gash cut into it. The controversial building has been called "violent" by one critic, "bold and sexy" by another.

WASHINGTON SQUARE ARCH

Washington Square North opposite Fifth Avenue
Built 1890-93, dedicated 1895
Architect: Stanford White

Once, what is now Washington Square was a paupers' burial ground, a "potters' field." It's believed that today as many as 20,000 bodies are buried beneath the cement and verdure of the nearly 10-acre square. It was also the site of public hangings, back when New York had such things and when the state penitentiary was located nearby on Christopher Street. (It later moved to Ossining, called Sing Sing, in Westchester County.)

Then in 1826 the city tidied up the site, put a fence around it, and called it the Washington Military Parade Ground. In the days before we built grand armories, with massive drill-halls, local militias needed spaces to practice their maneuvers, and open-air settings were provided. (Madison Square was another.) The drills were also public entertainments – as the hangings had been. Since the drills were not constant, the parade ground served most of the time as a public park. As Manhattan's population surged northward in the first half of the 19th century, the streets surrounding Washington Square, as the parade ground came to be known, enjoyed a period of high fashion. In the early 1830s, for example, elegant Greek Revival row houses, with high stoops, marble columns, and beautiful iron fences, were built along the north side of the square. It was in one of these dwellings that Henry James (who was

born in 1843 around the corner from here on Washington Place) set his classic novel *Washington Square*.

Though at this point the square's defining landmark had yet to be built. It was not until 1889, nine years after the publication of Henry James's novel, that an arch would ceremoniously mark the beginning of fabled Fifth Avenue – "taking its origin at this point," wrote Henry James, "with a spacious and confident air which already marked it for high destinies."

In April 1889, New York staged a major civic celebration of the centennial of George Washington's inauguration, in this city, as the nation's first president. President Benjamin Harrison reenacted Washington's arrival by boat on Manhattan Island. And the city erected a temporary triumphal arch, made of wood and plaster, a little to the north of Washington Square, straddling Fifth Avenue roughly at the line of Washington Mews, the stable alley directly behind the fine houses of Washington Square North. The architect of the arch was Stanford White, whose soon-to-open Madison Square Garden, on Madison Avenue and 26th Street, along with a few other works, had made him arguably the city's most famous architect. (He would soon be inarguably the most famous, and later still the most infamous.) New Yorkers, especially some of the old-

guard families that still lived in lower Fifth Avenue, liked White's arch so much that they said a permanent version of it should be made. To that end, a subscription was taken up, and in 1895 the permanent arch, 77 feet high and made of marble, was dedicated. The new arch was placed a little to the south, just inside of the square, but still right on the axis of Fifth Avenue.

The finest things about the arch artistically are without question the beautiful spandrel reliefs (in the triangular spaces to either side of the top of the arched opening). The winged figures, representing Peace and War, were the creations of sculptor Frederick MacMonnies, who also did the statuary groups on the Soldiers and Sailors Monument in Brooklyn and the fountains on the porch of the New York Public Library. Between 1914 and 1918 two over-life-size marble statues, with elaborate relief backings, were added to the north-facing piers of the arch. On the left is Washington as Commander-in-Chief by Hermon Atkins MacNeil; on the right is Washington as President by Alexander Stirling Calder. Nearly a century of coal smoke, auto exhaust fumes, and the corrosive droppings of pigeons did heavy damage to the arch, but a major restoration was done and the arch was triumphantly rededicated in 2004.

Washington Square in 1895 was very different from the square in the 1840s. A few of the old patrician families had hung on, to be sure. But the area to the south of the Square had become an Italian immigrant neighborhood in which the old town houses had been razed for tenements. (Many Italian restaurants and cafés continue to flourish in the area.) Elsewhere around the square, cheap rents (yes, cheap rents) and picturesque houses attracted "bohemians," the adventuresome, artistically inclined, often politically radical young people who would for many years define Greenwich Village in the popular imagination. Indeed, the arch itself came to be associated with Greenwich Village bohemian life. In 1917, a group led by the artists Marcel Duchamp and John Sloan, and the poet Gertrude Drick ascended to the top of the arch to proclaim "the free and independent state of Greenwich Village." In the 1950s and 1960s the arch formed the backdrop for impromptu concerts by folk singers, for poetry readings by Beat Generation luminaries and others, and for political protests.

As the neighborhood experiences further changes – today it is dominated by the campus of New York University and by high-end housing – the arch, as it has now done for well more than a century, continues to bear witness.

JEFFERSON MARKET COURTHOUSE

Sixth Avenue and 10th Street
Built 1874-77
Architects: Frederick Clarke Withers and Calvert Vaux

Originally the Third Judicial District Courthouse, this building exemplifies changing perceptions over time. When it was built, and for a short time thereafter, this was considered by professionals to be one of the most beautiful buildings in America. In its tortured forms, its wildly varied skyline, the strikingly contrasting colors of its materials, its distinctive high tower like a Medieval sentinel over Manhattan, and its relief carvings of scenes from *A Midsummer Night's Dream*, this courthouse was the *ne plus ultra* of the Victorian dream of elsewhere, of retreat to a distant, happier, cleaner, and more natural past.

And then the 20th century happened, and Victoriana became deeply unfashionable. Cities all over America faced little or no opposition in knocking down their Victorian buildings. After the Jefferson Market Courthouse closed in 1945, it seemed that this building, which only 70 or so years earlier had been voted by architects as one of the five most beautiful in the country, would, like so many of its benighted Victorian brethren, succumb to the wrecker's ball.

The name "Jefferson Market" comes from a long-ago food market established on this site in 1833. The market included a tall fire lookout tower. In the 1870s the new courthouse was built, along with new market sheds to its south and a jail building to the south and west. This was probably as fine an ensemble of Victorian buildings as was ever built in New York. The architectural harmony was ruined in 1929 when the market sheds and jail were replaced by an Art Deco high-rise, the Women's House of Detention, tall and bulky enough to overwhelm the adjacent courthouse, which at least escaped demolition.

By 1945 the courthouse was no longer needed by the city, and was abandoned. The building stood empty for a number of years, a deteriorating, rat-infested hulk of unloved Victoriana. But it was not unloved by everyone. Several Village women, led by Margot Gayle, Ruth Wittenberg, and Verna Small, fought plans for the demolition of the building and prevailed upon New York Mayor Robert Wagner to authorize the conversion of the building. Between 1965 and 1967 the architect Giorgio Cavaglieri expertly renovated the courthouse into the Jefferson Market Library. The Women's House of Detention was demolished in 1974, and the high tower (inspired by Ludwig II's Neuschwanstein Castle in Germany) again stood tall above Greenwich Village.

FLATIRON BUILDING

23rd Street at the intersection of Fifth Avenue and Broadway
Built 1902
Architect: D.H. Burnham & Co.

When the Flatiron Building was completed in 1902, women wore dresses that went down to the tops of their shoes. The Flatiron Building, because of its unusual triangular plan and the even more unusual fact that the building stands all alone on its own traffic island, created strong downdrafts that caused dresses to billow outward and expose women's ankles. Men routinely loitered in front of the building in the hope of catching a glimpse of ankle!

Such stories are legion when it comes to the Flatiron Building. Originally called the Fuller Building, it was quickly dubbed Flatiron for its resemblance to a clothing iron. The building, never the city's tallest, was nonetheless its most prominent, poised right at the crossing of Manhattan's two most fabled thoroughfares, Fifth Avenue and Broadway. The building pointed to the north, seemingly a symbol of the city's restless, relentless northward, or "uptown," growth. The Flatiron became the very symbol of modernity and progress. It was famously photographed by Alfred Stieglitz and Edward Steichen, painted by Childe Hassam, described in prose by O. Henry, H.G. Wells, and Ford Madox Ford.

It was designed by the firm of Daniel H. Burnham, the Chicagoan whose architectural practice may, in 1902, have been the largest in the world. Burnham had, a decade earlier, been in charge of the Columbian Exposition in Chicago, the most famous world's fair ever held in America.

The Flatiron is also an outstanding example of what we call the "tripartite skyscraper." In the early days of sky-scrapers, from the 1860s to the mid-1890s, architects were often defeated in their efforts to impose an aesthetically pleasing form on the new, outrageously tall, and awkward building type. But at the end of the century, such architects as Chicago's Louis Sullivan and New York's Bruce Price (see his nearby St. James Building on the southwest corner of Broadway and 26th Street) designed tall buildings with a distinct, heavily enriched base, a tall midsection, or shaft, in which just enough was done to relieve the oppressive fenestration, and a top (or, to use the analogy of a classical column, capital) that exploded in ornament, to define the building on the skyline. The Flatiron is faced in richly molded terra-cotta in an Italian Renaissance style. These surfaces combine with the triangular plan to produce a building of rare dynamism.

CHELSEA PIERS

Hudson River from West 17th to West 23rd Streets
Original Piers built 1902-07; present facility opened 1995

On April 18, 1912, the Cunard liner RMS *Carpathia* pulled into Pier 59, at West 19th Street in the great Chelsea Piers complex, to deposit the lifeboats that had held the survivors of RMS *Titanic*, which had so spectacularly sunk three days before on its maiden voyage from Southampton, England. The *Carpathia* continued to Pier 54, at West 13th Street, with the survivors (711 out of 2,224 who had been aboard the sunken ship) themselves. As for the *Titanic*, its destination had been Pier 60, at West 20th Street.

Extending from West 12th to West 22nd Streets, Chelsea Piers had been constructed between 1902 and 1907 to the designs of Warren & Wetmore, the architects of Grand Central Terminal, at a time when a whole new pier

infrastructure was needed to handle the new class of super-liners, like the *Titanic*, that were going into operation. The Piers handled the most glamorous of the luxury liners, including the *Mauretania* and the *Lusitania*. The latter departed from Pier 54 of the Chelsea Piers on May 1, 1915; on May 7, the famed liner was torpedoed by a German U-boat, and sank, with a death toll comparable to that of the *Titanic*.

After World War II, and the rise of commercial air travel, the ocean liner business declined. No longer a necessity, the great liners that continued to operate went into the specialty cruise business. Chelsea Piers was rebuilt in the early 1960s. The renovation eradicated all traces of Warren & Wetmore's grand design. And

it was all for nought: The Piers closed in 1968.

The decline in New York City of shipping and waterfront industry in the 1950s and 1960s left vast tracts of waterfront land vacant and moldering. It took a while, but eventually the city's waterfronts have found new uses. Often, as with Hudson River Park, which extends to the north and south

of Chelsea Piers, the new use is public parkland. At Chelsea Piers, it's a private development: the country's largest sports and recreation complex.

The 30-acre Chelsea Piers Sports and Entertainment Complex was opened by Roland W. Betts and Tom A. Bernstein (producers of the films *Pretty Woman* and *The Little Mermaid*) in 1995 in the disused piers between West 17th and West 23rd Streets. At first all they wanted to do was to build an ice hockey facility to handle overflow from the intensively used Sky Rink on Tenth Avenue and 31st Street. But the concept grew.

Today, Chelsea Piers, which has grown to become one of the most popular attractions in New York, includes two ice hockey rinks, a golf club, batting cages, basketball courts, bowling alleys, a health club, lacrosse and soccer fields, a swimming pool, a sand volleyball court, a rock climbing wall, and much more – including a brewpub. There is also a major television studio, where *Law & Order* was made.

IAC BUILDING

Eleventh Avenue between 18th and 19th Streets
Built 2007
Architect: Frank Gehry

His Guggenheim Museum (1997) in Bilbao, Spain, and his Walt Disney Concert Hall (2003) in Los Angeles, have arguably made Frank Gehry the most famous living architect in the world – and the most famous since Frank Lloyd Wright. It took a while for Gehry to design anything in New York. The Toronto-born architect has lived for more than half a century in southern California, where he also received his training. His aesthetic, in other words, came out of a place very different from New York. His first New York works were interiors: the Condé Nast cafeteria

(2000) and the Issey Miyake boutique (2001). Finally, in 2007 his first building here was completed, the headquarters of Barry Diller's InterActiveCorp. This is a holding company for a large number of popular web sites, including Match.com, Citysearch, and the Daily Beast.

It's hard for even Gehry's detractors to think the IAC Building is not the right building in the right place. This far western edge of Chelsea was until recently a largely derelict industrial district of nondescript buildings and roaring automobile traffic. Architecturally, there was, as Gertrude Stein once said of Oakland, "no there there." Thanks to Gehry, there is now a "there" on Eleventh Avenue. The ICA Building's undulating facades have been likened to a billowing pleated skirt, and the jagged, mountainous form to an iceberg. Gehry used more than 1400 unique, custom-made glass panels, "fritted" with white ceramic dots. He achieves his unusual sloping, torquing shapes using proprietary design software based on a program originally created to aid designers of airplanes. In the lobby, and visible from the West Side Highway, is a 140-foot-long, eleven-foot-high video wall that makes the building appear, especially at night, as though it is in motion. Gehry has since adorned New York with a second building, the 76-story 8 Spruce Street apartment building (see page 52).

100 ELEVENTH AVENUE

Northeast corner of 19th Street
Built 2008
Architect: Ateliers Jean Nouvel

Note next door the distinctive apartment building, 100 Eleventh Avenue, by the famous French architect Jean Nouvel. This recently placeless part of Manhattan is changing rapidly, in part because of the High Line. The Nouvel building uses more than 1700 glass panels that, like those of the IAC Building, are each unique in size and angle of placement. Though each panel is the same color, each catches the light differently, so that the building seems a riot of varied hues. Nouvel says he was inspired by the stained-glass art of Medieval cathedrals, and it's easy to see this. It's also easy to see what one critic said: The building is like a tight sequined dress.

WHITNEY MUSEUM OF AMERICAN ART

99 Gansevoort Street
Built 2011-15
Architect: Renzo Piano

The Whitney Museum of American Art was founded in 1931 by Gertrude Vanderbilt Whitney and Juliana Force. Mrs. Whitney had grown up in a 137-room mansion on Fifth Avenue and 57th Street (where Bergdorf-Goodman now is), but as an adult became a fine sculptor (see, for example, her statue of Peter Stuyvesant in Stuyvesant Square) and sought the company of artists in Greenwhich Village. One of the richest women in America (her parents' summer "cottage" was the Newport, Rhode Island, house known as The Breakers), she married one of the richest men, Harry Payne Whitney. But she divided her life between her role as society hostess on an estate in Westbury, and the bohemian life she enjoyed living and working in a converted stable in MacDougal Alley. She never stinted in her financial support of living American artists, and offered her vast collection of American paintings to the Metropolitan Museum of Art. When the Met, incredibly, rejected her offer, Mrs. Whitney hired the architect Auguste Noël to transform three row houses at 8 – 12 West 8th Street (directly behind her stable) into the first Whitney Museum of American Art. Now the prestigious New York Studio School of Drawing, Painting, and Sculpture, the building is one of the most delightfully eccentric structures in New York. When the museum outgrew the space it moved, in 1954, to a new building by Noel's firm on the site adjacent to the Museum of Modern Art, on 54th Street between Fifth and Sixth Avenues, and then, in 1966 to fancy Madison Avenue, at 75th Street, and a startling building – like an upside-down ziggurat sheathed in rich Canadian granite, with a "moat" – designed by Marcel Breuer. The museum once again outgrew itself and for many years tried to expand without success the 75th Street location.

It was decided to relocate the museum downtown in the industrial "Meat-Packing" District across from the entrance of The High Line. The new museum vastly increases the exhibition and programming space with the largest column-free gallery space in the city. Responding to the industrial character of the neighborhood, the strong and striking asymmetrical design features a dramatic cantilevered entrance which shelters a large public plaza. At this gathering place visitors see through the building entrance and the large windows to the Hudson River beyond. The Whitney is known for its Biennial survey of contemporary American avant-garde art, its Independent Study Program that has nurtured the careers of many young artists, and a collection that includes works by artists ranging from Albert Pinkham Ryder and Charles Burchfield to Andy Warhol and Cindy Sherman.

THE HIGH LINE

Gansevoort to 30th Streets, roughly along Tenth Avenue
Built 2006-11
Architects: Diller Scofidio + Renfro and Field Operations

For most of the 19th and 20th centuries, the West Side waterfront of Manhattan was one of the busiest port and terminal complexes on earth. Great steamships docked at Chelsea Piers and elsewhere along the riverfront. Countless barges, lighters, and carfloats came across the Hudson River from New Jersey. Their cargoes were then shifted to the warehouses and factories up and down the river by a waterfront freight railroad. For most of its history, this railroad ran at street level. Persistent calls from those who lived and worked nearby to make the railroad less obtrusive and less dangerous by elevating it or submerging it finally bore fruit as part of the vast West Side Improvement choreographed by master planner Robert Moses in the 1930s. This project doubled the size of Riverside Park, created the world-famous Henry Hudson Parkway and the Miller Highway, and gave us the High Line – the elevated tracks used by the freight trains of the New York Central Railroad.

The High Line opened in 1934, connecting the vast freight yards at 34th Street to the St. John's Park Terminal at Spring Street. It was designed to serve the factories and warehouses along its path as efficiently

as possible, and so it was threaded among the buildings of the waterfront and, dramatically, sent right through some buildings. Among the great industrial concerns that the High Line served were the Nabisco bakery, once the world's largest bakery, where the Oreo cookie was invented, and the Bell Labs, where work was done on many of the defining inventions of the 20th century including the transistor and the laser. Today, the Nabisco plant has been transformed into a wonderful food market and TV studio complex called Chelsea Market, and the Bell Labs have become a subsidized housing complex for artists called Westbeth.

What about the High Line? The trains stopped running in 1980. The part south of Gansevoort Street had already been decommissioned and demolished, in the 1960s. The rest awaited demolition, as well. Even though some local business owners felt the old railroad viaduct to be a blight on a neighborhood with a lot of commercial potential, there was no real urgency in taking it down. Over the years, many people became fascinated by it: fascinated by its history, by its ghostly presence, and by how nature had claimed it, as riotously colorful wildflowers had crowded the old train bed. Though it was illegal to climb up for a look, lots of people did. The renowned photographer Joel Meyerowitz even made a book of photos from it.

In 1999 Robert Hammond and Joshua David formed a group called Friends of the High Line. Their vision was to turn it into an elevated park, like the Promenade Plantée, a park built atop a disused railroad viaduct in Paris. Their idea gained traction, and the support of Mayor Bloomberg, and so construction began in 2006. The architects Diller Scofidio + Renfro, the landscape architects Field Operations, and star gardener Piet Oudolf created a dazzling park, combining restored elements of the railroad operations with plantings relating to the native ecology of the area.

Builders and architects on nearby streets also got into the act: The High Line became something of an architectural theme park, with such works as the Polshek Partnership's Standard Hotel straddling the park itself, and such notable buildings as Jean Nouvel's 100 Eleventh Avenue and

Frank Gehry's IAC Building clearly visible from the park walkways. The new Whitney Museum of American Art (see page 78) has opened at the

southern end, where the park terminates in the chic meatpacking district. Phase 1 of the park, from Gansevoort to 20th Streets, opened in June 2009; phase 2, from 20th to 30th Streets, opened in June 2011.

It is the biggest attraction in New York.

EMPIRE STATE BUILDING

Fifth Avenue between 33rd and 34th Streets
Built 1929-1931
Architect: William Lamb (1883-1952)

In 1945 a U.S. Army Air Corps B-25 bomber flew off course in a storm and weaved among the skyscrapers of midtown Manhattan – until the plane crashed into the 79th floor of the north face of the Empire State Building. The U.S. was at the time still at war with Japan, and the press had speculated on the possibility of attacks on American cities. People at first thought the crash was a deliberate attack on an American icon.

The icon was the tallest building in the world. The Empire State Building had been the tallest for fourteen years, since overtopping the Chrysler Building in 1931. Through the Great Depression and World War II we had stopped building tall buildings, and no one knew when – or if – we would resume. In fact, not until the 1970s would a building rise higher than the Empire State, though today it only just still ranks in the top 20 tallest buildings in the world. The Burj Khalifa, in Dubai, is more than twice as high as the Empire State Building.

And yet the 1,250-foot-high, 102-story Empire State Building is still as likely as not the automatic answer to the question "What's the world's tallest building?" That's probably because it held the title for four decades, longer by far than any other skyscraper.

The high stainless steel spire that surmounts the Art Deco tower was, amazingly, designed as a mooring mast for dirigibles – the airships once thought to represent the future of air travel. The Empire State's developers indulged a futuristic fantasy of giant airships hovering and docking right over Midtown, the passengers alighting onto the roof of the world's tallest building. As it happens, only two such dockings took place, both shortly after the building's completion. The practical problems of docking dirigibles more than a thousand feet above ground proved nettlesome enough that the idea was scrapped.

Developed by John J. Raskob, who as the longtime public face of General Motors and chairman of the Democratic National Committee was

one of the best-known figures
associated with the Roaring Twenties
in America, and designed by William
Lamb of Shreve, Lamb & Harmon, the
Empire State was a speculative office
building erected a little to the south of
the main office district of midtown.
The site became available to Raskob
and his investing partners when the
fabled Waldorf-Astoria Hotel, which
had been located there since the 1890s,
sought to move from a part of town
that had become unfashionable for
hotels. When the deal was made, the
Waldorf moved to its present location
on Park Avenue, and the old hotel was
demolished, one New York icon
yielding to another.

THE MORGAN LIBRARY

Madison Avenue between 36th and 37th Streets
Built 1906 (library on 36th Street), 2006 (Renzo Piano addition)
Architects: McKim, Mead & White (1906), Renzo Piano (2006)

The Morgan Library is one of the most fascinating museums in the world. Generally, it is not a place for exhibitions of paintings, or for blockbusters. The shows tend to be specialized, small, intimate, and scholarly. The Morgan's specialty is rare books, manuscripts, and works on paper – Gutenberg Bibles (three of them, more than any other institution in the world), Medieval and Renaissance illuminated manuscripts, autograph manuscripts by great writers and composers, master drawings, etc.

In the 1850s, just as Murray Hill was becoming the fashionable neighborhood in Manhattan, members of the Phelps and Dodge families (who were in business with one another) erected three large brownstone mansions along the east side of Madison Avenue between 36th and 37th Streets. These were all eventually purchased by John Pierpont Morgan, the most powerful banker in New York – perhaps the most powerful individual in Wall Street's history. The southernmost brownstone was Morgan's and his wife's own residence. The northernmost he gave to his son, Jack Morgan. The middle house he tore down to create a garden. Meanwhile, the elder Morgan's collecting mania had gone into overdrive. Many of the greatest treasures of the Metropolitan Museum of Art (of which Morgan was

president) and the Frick Collection were once owned by Morgan. What he kept closest to him, though, were his books and manuscripts. And in 1906 Charles McKim of McKim, Mead & White built a wing onto Morgan's house, to the east on 36th Street. The elegant and refined marble structure was Morgan's private library. It's also where in 1907 he locked up all the most powerful bankers and financiers in America until they could hash out a plan to avert a financial catastrophe.

Morgan died in 1913. In the 1920s, Jack Morgan demolished his father's house and replaced it with a new structure that, together with the library on 36th Street, would function as a public museum of his father's book and manuscript collections. In the 1980s the museum purchased Jack Morgan's old house, on Madison and 37th, and added it to the complex by roofing over the in-between garden with glass. Not content to stop there, in 2006 the museum replaced this with a new, dramatic glass atrium by the world-renowned architect Renzo Piano. This added important new gallery space, an auditorium, underground storage, and other facilities, and tied together the three older structures. The Morgan Library & Museum is now an interlocking complex of buildings, each with a distinctive architectural character and each well worth exploring.

TIMES SQUARE (and Father Duffy Square)

Broadway, 42nd to 47th Streets
Times Tower (One Times Square)
built 1904
Architect of Times Tower: Cyrus L.W.
Eidlitz

Where Broadway, which cuts a diagonal across the Manhattan street grid, crosses Seventh Avenue it forms an X in the street plan. This leaves two of those triangular traffic islands New Yorkers call squares: To the south, from 42nd to 43rd Streets, is Times Square, the triangle where the One Times Square Building (formerly Times Tower) stands; to the north, from 46th to 47th Streets, is Father Duffy Square, named for (and bearing a statue of) Francis Patrick Duffy, the Roman Catholic priest known for his bravery in World War I. New Yorkers and visitors tend to call both "squares," as well as the adjacent streets, by the name of "Times Square."

Once it was Longacre Square, a center of the carriage-making industry. In 1904, newspaper publisher Adolph Ochs moved his *New York Times* from Park Row, near City Hall, to Longacre Square. He built the Times Tower, a distinctive, triangular-plan, completely freestanding skyscraper. Though *The Times* only remained in the building until 1913, the city renamed Longacre Square to Times Square. Today One Times Square is largely unoccupied: The facades are completely obscured by large electric advertisements and, it turns out, the building is more valuable as a carriage for advertising

signs than as an office building.

Around the same time the *New York Times* moved to the neighborhood, the Theater District began moving uptown. By World War I, Times Square had become the new Theater District, and had a raffish glamour to it. It also was one of the greatest nighttime displays on earth. Successive New York theater districts had been known as the "Great

White Way" for their illumination by white-glowing electric lights. In the 1920s, Times Square added dazzlingly colored neon signs, creating an urban spectacle like no other. So important were the signs to the identity of Times Square that when the neighborhood underwent redevelopment in the 1990s as a new center of corporate headquarters, civic groups such as the venerable Municipal Art Society, long known for fighting against advertisements and billboards, successfully advocated that the city make a law requiring large, illuminated advertisements on all new buildings in the area. Times Square must be the only place on earth where loud advertising signs are not just permitted, but are *required*, by law.

NEW YORK PUBLIC LIBRARY

Fifth Avenue between 40th and 42nd Streets
Built 1899-1911
Architects: Carrère & Hastings

New York Public Library system was created at the end of the 19th century, and the main library, on Fifth Avenue between 40th and 42nd Streets – known to most New Yorkers as the "42nd Street Library" – opened in 1911. The system comprises many specialized collections dispersed among several locations. The 42nd Street library – now called the Stephen A. Schwarzman Building after the hedge-fund billionaire donated $100 million to the library, its largest gift ever – houses the humanities and social sciences research collections. These collections are rivaled in the United States only by the Library of Congress in Washington, D.C. Indeed, New York's is by far the largest municipal library in the world, comparable only to the great national libraries.

It is suitably housed in one of Manhattan's very grandest edifices. Designed by John Merven Carrère and Thomas Hastings in close consultation with the founding librarian Dr. John Shaw Billings, the library stretches across two full blocks of Fifth Avenue. A splendid balustraded terrace wraps around the building, blending round the west side of the building into Bryant Park. The facade is of Vermont marble, which now gleams following a

thorough exterior restoration of the building on the occasion of its 100th birthday. On the library's porch note especially the outstanding bronze flagpole bases at either end of the terrace, probably the finest examples of their kind in the country; they were cast by Tiffany Studios. The fountains – one called "Truth," the other "Beauty" – by the great American sculptor Frederick MacMonnies, on either side of the portico, are similarly as good as one will find in the whole country. The famous stone lions were designed by the animalier Edward Clark Potter (who also gave us the pair of lionesses in front of the Morgan Library on 36th Street just east of Madison Avenue); during the Great Depression, Mayor Fiorello La Guardia nicknamed the lions "Patience" and "Fortitude," the two strengths New Yorkers needed to endure the tough times. New Yorkers have long been fond of saying that when you study at the library, you are "reading between the lions."

Co-architect John Carrère was tragically killed in an automobile accident two months before the building opened to the public; the library trustees felt it only right that his body should lay in state in the library.

Inside, the Astor Hall is a rare all-stone room in which floor, walls, and ceiling are entirely of marble. There are so many interior marvels that they cannot be listed here, but do visit the Gottesman Exhibition Hall, which has one of the most beautiful ceilings in America, and, on the third floor, the magnificent Rose Main Reading Room, which stretches the width of the building, and is as sumptuously appointed as any room in New York. The Reading Room, and the library as a whole, is open to everyone: The collections and the building's decoration make this the people's palace.

GRAND CENTRAL TERMINAL

42nd Street opposite Park Avenue
Built 1903-13
Architects: Reed & Stem and Warren & Wetmore

"Crossroads of a million private lives!" as the old radio series used to say – half a million people pass through Grand Central Terminal every day. It's much more than just a train station: It's a shopping and dining destination, a shortcut for pedestrians, a "mixing chamber" at the hub of subway lines, interurban trains, and vehicular roadways. And it's one of the most beautiful buildings in New York.

Built on the site of an earlier station after the New York Central Railroad decided to switch its operations from steam to electrical power, Grand Central is an underground facility with two sub-terranean levels of tracks. Tracks and yards spread out below ground from Madison to Lexington Avenues and from 42nd to 50th Streets; the magnificent building on 42nd Street opposite Park Avenue is just the "tip of the iceberg." But what a tip! The sculpture, "The Glory of Commerce," that crowns the 42nd Street facade, shows us Mercury, Roman god of commerce and transportation, flanked by Hercules (strength) and Minerva (wisdom). It may be the finest monumental sculpture in America. Its sculptor, Jules-Félix Coutan, created a plaster maquette in his Paris studio. In Long Island City, Queens, the peerless carvers Donnelly and Ricci, guided by Coutan's maquette, crafted the final, full-size version, fifteen hundred tons (it's true!) of solid Indiana limestone, that was

shipped to 42nd Street and hoisted into place atop the building sixteen months after the terminal's opening.

An elevated roadway wraps around the building, forming a kind of terrace or platform. This rises from and descends to Park Avenue, which Grand Central straddles. By tightly belting the structure with this roadway, the architects cleverly avoided slicing a tunnel through the building, which would have compromised their ability to create majestic interior spaces.

And speaking of majestic interiors, the Main Concourse is one of the city's most wondrous rooms. The great barrel-vaulted space not only has breathtaking scale, but is also superbly designed with cast-stone walls, cocoa-colored Bottocino marble accents, a floor of Tennessee Pink marble, and a blue-green ceiling that all blend into a soothing mood. Upon entering this space one feels that great burdens have been lifted from one's shoulders. What more can we ask of architecture?

The "Sky Ceiling" mural, cresting at 120 feet, shows the mythological characterizations of the constellations. Observers note that the constellations appear in reverse, but the designers based the mural on an old manuscript painting that depicted the cosmos from God's point of view, outside the celestial sphere, so that indeed it is all the reverse of what we see from earth. The idea for the mural came from the

celebrated French painter Paul Helleu but was executed by J. Monroe Hewlett and Charles Basing. Thirty years later it had significantly decayed and was repainted by Charles Gulbrandsen. Half a century of cigarette smoke so darkened the mural that when it was cleaned in the 1990s it was a stunning revelation.

In the 1990s the terminal underwent an extensive rehabilitation by the architects Beyer Blinder Belle. The place

had been falling apart for decades, covered in grime and gaudy advertisements. The lofty ramps connecting upper and lower levels had been roofed and turned into dank tunnels, and blackout paint applied to windows during World War II had never been cleaned away. The years-long renovation made Grand Central sparkle like new, and symbolized, as did nothing else, the new spirit of a city that had not long before appeared to be dying.

METLIFE BUILDING (200 Park Avenue)

45th Street opposite Park Avenue
Built 1963
Architects: Emery Roth & Sons with Walter Gropius and Pietro Belluschi

For many years this was one of the most unloved buildings in Manhattan. Originally called the Pan Am Building, it was designed by Emery Roth & Sons, a firm responsible for the design of fully half of all the office space built in Manhattan between 1950 and 1970. But in this case developer Erwin Wolfson hired two of the "starchitects" of the early 1960s, the German Walter Gropius, dean of the school of architecture at Harvard, and the Italian Pietro Belluschi, head of the architecture school at the Massachusetts Institute of Technology. Surely these talents would give the city one of its iconic buildings.

And the Pan Am did become an icon. When opened in 1963 it was the largest (but not the tallest) office building that had ever been built, with more than three million square feet of floor area. However, its extraordinary bulk, plus the way it obliterated the once beautiful Park Avenue vista, caused many New Yorkers to detest the new building.

In recent years, a younger generation that never knew Park Avenue before the MetLife Building does not dislike it at all. In fact, the way the building enhances pedestrian flow into and out of the Main Concourse of Grand Central Terminal is celebrated. The reversal of opinion may not be as dramatic as happened with the nearby Chrysler Building (generally disliked when it was built, universally loved today), but it is another good example of how every building has its day. Though now almost 40 years old, the building, with its enormous floor-plates, still admirably suits the needs of modern corporate tenants, who also like it because of its unmatched location.

When built, the Pan Am Building had a rooftop heliport. But in 1977 all helicopter operations ceased after a terrible accident in which a whirling helicopter blade broke off and flew into a crowd of waiting passengers, killing four, and then dropped 55 stories onto the street below, killing a pedestrian. On an altogether happier note, in recent years a pair of peregrine falcons (listed as an endangered species, 1970-1999) has nested on the 58th floor of the MetLife Building. The falcons found city life to their liking: Food (other birds) was plentiful, and the tops and sides of skyscrapers resembled the birds' favored mountain eyries. In 2011 there were believed to be more than 30 adult peregrine falcons resident in the city. Two peregrine falcons (nicknamed "Lois" and "Clark"), at least, are glad the MetLife Building is there.

CHRYSLER BUILDING

42nd Street and Lexington Avenue
Built 1928-30
Architect: William Van Alen

The great, stainless steel Mycenaean helmet that tops the Chrysler Building emerged on the afternoon of October 23, 1929 – the day before "Black Thursday" – from within the shell of the building's shaft. Stunned passersby watched the pointy spire rise, then settle into place.

This theatrical stunt was the culmination of the famous competition to claim the title of The World's Tallest Building. In one corner were architects H. Craig Severance and Yasuo Matsui with their 68-storey design for the Bank of Manhattan Trust Building (40 Wall Street); in the other corner, Severance's former partner, William Van Alen, commissioned by automaker Walter Chrysler to design an office building in the heart of what was fast becoming the new central business district of Manhattan. Cunningly, Severance added 3 stories to his building, and at 927ft announced to the world's press the building's claim to the title of world's tallest building. But not to be outdone Van Alen got Chrysler to agree to the addition of the distinctive Chrysler crown, which was assembled secretly within the walls of the building itself. The surprise spire earned the Chrysler building the coveted title and Van Alen, his nickname: the Ziegfeld of architecture. His triumph was short-lived, however: barely a year later, the Empire State Building, built by a longtime rival of

Walter Chrysler, rose significantly higher than Van Alen's building and stole the title.

The Chrysler – the first building ever to rise higher than Paris's Eiffel Tower, and the first man-made structure to rise above 1,000 feet – is, by 2011, just the 50th tallest building in the world. But if no longer famous for being tall, the Chrysler is famous for being one of the most exquisite Art Deco buildings ever erected. The crown, whether glinting in afternoon sun light, or with its triangular windows illuminated at night, is still the most conspicuous, and beloved, object on the Manhattan skyline.

The lobby, however, is for most people the building's *raison d'être*. Triangular in shape, slightly delirious in the way of a German Expressionist stage set, the lobby is a feast of rare materials and exotic patterns. The walls are of rouge flamme marble from Morocco. All the lighting is indirect, reflected off panels of polished Mexican

onyx. And the elevators, with doors of elaborate wood marquetry and each with a unique cab design, are the most celebrated in New York. The Chrysler Building management is to be commended for welcoming visitors into the lobby, bucking the trend in which some buildings have made lobby access a perquisite of building tenancy.

Interestingly, the Chrysler was hardly universally loved when it was built. Many people – public and pro-fessionals alike – felt it was a little over-the-top, and objected to the blatant incorporation of Chrysler motorcar imagery in the building's iconography – the "gargoyles", for example, were based on Chrysler radiator caps – that, some said, turned the skyscraper into a giant billboard. More recently, however, an international poll of architects named the Chrysler the second most important work of architecture of the 20th century.

THE UNITED NATIONS HEADQUARTERS

First Avenue between 42nd and 48th Streets
Built 1947-52
Architects: Wallace K. Harrison and an
international committee of ten architects

It was not preordained that New York would be the home of the new "world government" founded in the aftermath of the Second World War. Other cities vied passionately to get the headquarters. But New Yorker Nelson Rockefeller, grandson of the richest American who ever lived, made an improbable eleventh-hour deal to acquire for the United Nations just the plot of midtown Manhattan land to meet the organization's every fancy. To do so he had had to track down the plot's owner, the prominent real-estate developer William Zeckendorf, at the Stork Club, a fabled nightspot on East 52nd Street, in the wee small hours of the morning and get the tipsy tycoon to sign the necessary documents. Then Rockefeller had to prevail upon the all-powerful public-works czar of New York, Robert Moses, to push through the needed legislative approvals, complicatedly transferring the land out of the possession of the United States, at record speed.

It should thus come as no surprise that Rockefeller's close friend, architect Wallace K. Harrison, was then placed in charge of the design. An international committee of ten architects consulted on the plans; the final design we credit largely to the Brazilian Oscar Niemeyer (architect of the capital city of Brasília), modified by Le Corbusier, the legendary Swiss-born French designer.

The complex that emerged includes the 39-story Secretariat Building, the first glass-curtain-wall tower in New York. The great slab, set beside the East River, shining a silvery blue in the slanting sun, sometimes nearly blindingly so, was an architectural image entirely new to New York. The Secretariat Building houses the offices of the Secretary-General (the eighth and current one being Ban Ki-moon of South Korea) and the large U.N. staff that carries out the directives of the General Assembly, the Security Council, and other deliberative bodies within the

organization. The Secretariat Building is where the U.N. bureaucracy resides.

The Secretariat tower forms a distinctive composition with the low-lying, scooping General Assembly Building. The inside, with its swooping white ramps, and the great, domed assembly chamber with its Scandinavian woodiness and two murals by Fernand Léger (and seating for 1800), defines postwar taste as do few other sets of interiors in the city. The General Assembly comprises all member states, of which there are currently 192. The Security Council, comprising five permanent and ten non-permanent member states, meets in the "Norwegian Room," designed by Norway's Arnstein Arneberg, in the Conference Building. Situated between the Secretariat and the General Assembly, the Conference Building is the third of the original three United Nations buildings.

The complex features gardens and open spaces, adorned with artworks, and, along First Avenue, a display of flags of all member states, arranged alphabetically, from Afghanistan to Zimbabwe.

NEW YORK YACHT CLUB

37 West 44th Street
Built 1899-1900
Architects: Warren & Wetmore

America's most prestigious sailing club was founded by nine rich yachting enthusiasts in 1844. The group was led by John Cox Stevens, who was sworn in as Commodore (as the club calls its president) aboard his yacht, *Gimcrack*. (Stevens was the son of Colonel John Stevens, the founder of Hoboken, New Jersey.) Two days after the club's founding, its members set sail from the Battery to Newport, Rhode Island – the New York Yacht Club's other home. The club most famously has held the America's Cup trophy for most of its history. In 1851 a schooner called *America* won a race, sponsored by the Royal Yacht Squadron (Britain's most famous yacht club), around the Isle of Wight (home of the Royal Yacht Squadron). The trophy awarded to America was named for the boat. The trophy then went on display at the recently formed New York Yacht Club, the home club of *America*. Any yacht club in the world that meets certain standards has the right to challenge for the Cup. It so happens that the New York Yacht Club held on to the Cup from 1851 to 1983 – a streak to put the New York Yankees to shame! In 1983 the Cup was taken by the Royal Perth Yacht Club of Australia. Since then, the New York Yacht Club has failed to retrieve the Cup. It currently resides at the Golden Gate Yacht Club in San Francisco.

From 1901 to 1983 the trophy was proudly displayed in the building that remains home to the New York Yacht Club. Located on 44th Street between Fifth and Sixth Avenues, just to the west of the Harvard Club (there is a little overlap in membership between the two clubs), the building, designed by Warren & Wetmore, is one of the most wonderful Beaux-Arts structures in the city. It is well worth the detour to see, all the more so if you find a club member to invite you inside as his or her guest.

There is no other building facade like this one in New York. Warren & Wetmore was one of New York's greatest architectural firms, responsible for such masterpieces as Grand Central Terminal. The New York Yacht Club features one of the firm's characteristically beautiful classical compositions. But here they add one of the most fanciful things to be found in the city: the set of three high-arched carved-stone window bays in the form of galleon sterns that send cascades of water – carved in limestone – over the building's base. These windows look in on the Club's Model Room, a space containing beautiful models of members' boats. The room also features a carved-stone fireplace surround that rises all the way to the top of the double-height ceiling, and a gallery, of exquisitely carved woodwork, wrapping around the top of the room. For good measure, there is a lovely stained-glass skylight. It is one of the city's most extraordinary rooms, in a building that has one of the most extraordinary facades.

RADIO CITY MUSIC HALL

Sixth Avenue and 50th Street
Built 1932
Architects: Edward Durell Stone and Donald Deskey

When John D. Rockefeller Jr. built Rockefeller Center in the depths of the Depression he and his advisers had to apply considerable ingenuity to finding tenants for the world's largest business complex. People still read newspapers, so Rockefeller got Associates Press, and magazines (*Time-Life*), went to the movies (RKO) and, above all, listened to the radio (RCA and its subsidiary, the National Broadcasting Company). So identified with radio and with NBC did the Center become, that for years it was known as "Radio City." And so it was that the grand theater that was supposed to be called the International Music Hall was renamed Radio City Music Hall.

From 1932 until 1979 the Music Hall followed a format of presenting stage shows and films in the same program. The format was worked out by the Music Hall's original manager, Samuel "Roxy" Rothafel. Previously, Rothafel had been manager at the Roxy Theater (on West 50th Street between Sixth and Seventh Avenues, now sadly demolished) for five years, where he had developed a high-kicking, all-female precision dance team called the Roxyettes. When he moved to Radio City Music Hall, he brought the dancers

with him, and they were renamed the Rockettes. They are still a feature of the Music Hall. Indeed, the only feature of the Music Hall that competes in fame and glamour with the Rockettes is the architecture. It is one of the Art Deco masterpieces of the world. The Hall seats six thousand people, which made it the largest indoor theater in the world when it opened. The renowned Wurlitzer organ is the largest pipe organ ever made for a motion picture theater. The auditorium is a breathtaking space of curved, streamlined shapes. The lobby is just as thrilling, with its streamlined cylindrical chandeliers, chrome and mirrored accents, and the dramatic stairway mural by Ezra Winter. The exterior is by contrast relatively plain, but do look on the 50th Street side for the three lovely enamelled medallions – 'Dance', 'Drama' and 'Song' – by the artist Hildreth Meiere.

Radio City Music Hall is at its most crowded during the holiday season. It seems everyone in America comes to New York to see the Christmas tree in Rockefeller Plaza and to see the annual Magnificent Christmas Spectacular, starring the Rockettes, at Radio City Music Hall.

ROCKEFELLER CENTER & GE BUILDING

Fifth Avenue, 48th to 51st Streets
Built 1930-39
Architects: Associated Architects (led by Raymond Hood
followed by Wallace K. Harrison)

It was the 1920s, Manhattan real estate was booming, and John D. Rockefeller Jr. had a plan for his backyard. The Metropolitan Opera Company was, as it had been since 1883, in the old Met, on Broadway between 38th and 39th Streets. In 1883 that had been the glamorous Theater District. In the 1920s, it was the Garment District, and the Met wanted, badly, to move. They scouted potential locations until Rockefeller offered them a central site in a large new development he planned for the blocks just to the south of where he lived on West 54th Street. It was a neighborhood of old-fashioned brownstone houses, once fashionable, now a concentration of speakeasies (it was Prohibition), an area in need of "renewal." The new development, which would wipe away hundreds of brownstones between 48th and 51st Streets and Fifth and Sixth Avenues, was to be called Metropolitan Square – after the opera company.

But just as the plan was gestating, the stock market crash of 1929 changed things a bit. The Met could no longer sell its old building, and could not contribute its agreed-upon share to the building of the new opera house. Rockefeller decided to move ahead without the Met. And he moved ahead in the face of the storm that was the worst decade in the history of the American economy. But it was creative business planning that brought into being, and made – even in the depths of the Depression – a stunning success of what is to date (2011) the largest complex of business buildings ever erected.

Rockefeller had his pick of talent at a time when even the best architects and artists and construction people were desperate for work. It is seldom noted that the team he assembled included surprisingly many people who had an association with the late, great American architect Bertram Goodhue, who had died in 1924. Rockefeller hired Goodhue to design the Rockefeller Memorial Chapel at the University of Chicago. Rockefeller, who owned the Unicorn Tapestries and built the Cloisters, and Goodhue, a master of the Gothic Revival, were both lovers of the Middle Ages. If Goodhue had lived, perhaps he would have designed Rockefeller Center. Instead, the architects Raymond Hood and Wallace K. Harrison and the artists Lee Lawrie and Hildreth Meiere, who had worked for Goodhue, were among the principal creators of Rockefeller Center.

Rockefeller Center is unique. The buildings, as with Goodhue's later work, combine streamlined, "modernistic" forms with the solid feeling of traditional work. The first thirteen buildings of Rockefeller Center were built between 1930 and 1939, and are instantly identifiable by their uniform coatings of beautiful Indiana lime-

stone. Never before had skyscrapers
been laid out along the lines of a
formal, European-style town plan.
Never before had a soaring skyscraper,
such as the R.C.A. (now G.E.) Building,
30 Rockefeller Center, been placed at
the end of a long, axial vista – the
famed Promenade leading west off

Fifth Avenue. It is one of the most
thrilling vistas in New York.

The Promenade culminates at its
western end in a sunken plaza that was
originally meant to be the gateway to an
underground shopping center. That was
one of the few missteps in the original
plan. Rockefeller himself introduced

the idea of the ice skating rink, which in the colder months offers the most unusual and charming of Manhattan spectacles: In the midst of America's densest agglomeration of mega-business buildings is a fairy tale scene (as though in a clearing in the woods) of skaters going round and round.

The idea for the annual Christmas tree came from the original construction workers who put up a small tree to lend a little seasonal cheer to their work site. Rockefeller Center made it an annual event from the beginning, and during the holiday season there is no more visited site in the city.

SAINT PATRICK'S CATHEDRAL

Fifth Avenue between 50th and 51st Streets
Built 1858-79, towers completed 1888
Architect: James Renwick Jr.

New York City did not have enough Catholics to become an Archdiocese of the Roman Catholic Church until 1850. But because of the immigration of Irish and Germans around that time, Catholics soon came to dominate the city's population. The old cathedral, on Mott and Prince Streets, had opened in 1815, and needed to be replaced. The Church had acquired a country house on Fifth Avenue between 50th and 51st Streets with the thought of using it for a college. But that is where New York's fiery archbishop, John Hughes, decided to put the new cathedral. He further determined that the new cathedral should be the largest and most sumptuous building ever built in New York up to that time, a statement of pride and confidence by the city's poor and beleaguered Catholics. Hughes broke ground on Fifth Avenue in 1858, but did not live to see the completion of his brainchild, which opened in 1879, fifteen years after his death.

Designed by James Renwick Jr., an Episcopalian architect who had demonstrated his mastery of the Gothic style in such works as Grace Church, on Broadway and 10th Street, of 1846, St. Patrick's was by all odds the grandest ecclesiastical edifice in the country – and few buildings (the Capitol in Washington, D.C., comes to mind) of any kind were grander. Renwick's great

challenge was to shoehorn the cathedral into a single block of the Manhattan street grid – a constraint the builders of the great Medieval cathedrals had not had to face. He did so, however, with great imagination. He was unafraid to deviate from the norms of Gothic design – for example, his decision to forego the use of flying buttresses (which were structurally unnecessary but which a lesser architect would have put in anyway) – in order to harmonize the proportions dictated by the awkward site. Renwick's sure sense of proportion is evident nowhere more than in the high, graceful twin towers of the Fifth Avenue front. The 330-foot towers, completed in 1888, were for many years the tallest structures in New York – the original "twin towers." Their dramatic taper is unmatched in the world, not even by any of the great Medieval cathedrals.

The exterior of St. Patrick's is in the French Gothic style of Cologne Cathedral in Germany. Construction of Cologne Cathedral began in the 13th century, but the building was not completed until 1880. Architects were fascinated to watch the final phase of work of the great cathedral, begun in 1842 and based on the original plans. In the great 19th-century enthusiasm for all things Medieval, Cologne inspired

major churches in several cities, including Paris and Vienna as well as New York.

Inside, St. Patrick's follows more of an English style, immediately recognizable to anyone who has visited Westminster Abbey in London, or York Minster in Yorkshire. The interior soars in the best tradition of Gothic cathedrals, but the experience of a visit to St. Patrick's is not always what it should be. The interior is packed with pews, making maneuvering difficult, and always crowded with people. Also, the space, no doubt out of consideration for the vast crowds, is over-illuminated, which means one never experiences the full impact of the light filtering through the stained-glass windows.

That said, the cathedral has an encyclopedic collection of windows. The original 19th-century windows, visible in the aisles, though set in Gothic frames, were executed in a classical style, rendered in enamel paints. The handiwork mostly of the French glass master Nicolas Lorin, these are probably the best windows of their kind in the city. The clerestory windows, up above, are 20th-century windows by the Bostonian Charles Connick, a leader of a Medieval revival in stained glass. These use the "pot metal" technique of the Middle Ages, laying up pieces of integrally colored (not painted) glass in a mosaic technique to create the schematic, often abstract, imagery we associate with Medieval churches. Behind the altar is the beautiful Lady Chapel, added in 1906. Dedicated to the Virgin Mary, this chapel, with its great stained-glass walls, is reminiscent of Sainte-Chapelle in Paris, and is one of the most popular wedding sites in New York.

St. Patrick's was such a special building that it became a great source of pride not only for the city's Catholics, but for all New Yorkers.

VILLARD HOUSES &
NEW YORK PALACE HOTEL

Madison Avenue between 50th and 51st Streets
Built 1881-85
Architects: McKim, Mead & White

Ferdinand Heinrich Gustav Hilgard migrated from his native Bavaria to Illinois in 1853. He worked as a journalist, covered and supported Lincoln, and held abolitionist views. Then, in a totally 19th-century way, he woke up one morning to find himself president of the Northern Pacific Railroad. As a rich man, he moved to New York and indulged his political interests by purchasing the *New York Evening Post* and a magazine called *The Nation*.

Hilgard changed his name to Henry Villard and married the daughter of Boston abolitionist William Lloyd Garrison, who had family connections to Miller McKim, founder of *The Nation*. And so it was that when Villard decided to build on Madison Avenue he chose McKim, Mead & White, the fledgling firm of Miller McKim's son, Charles. Another famous partner in that firm was Stanford White (whose father wrote for the *Nation*), and White contributed much to the interiors. But the true author of the remarkable group of six houses was Joseph M. Wells. Wells, obsessively devoted to the architecture of the Italian High Renaissance (at a time when New York architecture was defined by such Victorian fantasies as the Jefferson Market Courthouse), gave Villard (and New York) a soberly beautiful exercise in elegant classicism. The houses are gathered into a single grand structure

that wraps around a generous courtyard. When built, in the early 1880s, the courtyard faced across Madison Avenue to another, similarly scaled courtyard behind St. Patrick's Cathedral; the St. Patrick's courtyard was later replaced by the cathedral's Lady Chapel.

Villard and his family lived in 451 Madison, now a restaurant called Gilt. Several of its rooms are among the very few interiors to be designated as New York City landmarks. The house's Music Room, now a bar, features dazzling murals by John La Farge and a vaulted, gilded ceiling of intricately swirling classical forms. Unfortunately for Villard, his railroad went bankrupt shortly after he built the houses, and he was forced to move. His house then became the longtime residence of Whitelaw Reid, editor and then publisher of the *New York Tribune*, and his family. This part of Midtown was once home to many rich families, who, as stores began to move in, migrated to the Upper East Side. In the late 1940s the Archdiocese of New York purchased four of what were by then five houses (two had been combined) for use as their administrative offices. The house across the courtyard from Villard's, 457 Madison, became the headquarters of the publisher Random House during the tenure of Bennett Cerf. In the 1970s the complex was acquired by real estate

developer Harry Helmsley, who incorporated three of the five houses into the high-rise Palace Hotel that he built abutting the houses to the east. For many years the distinguished civic organization the Municipal Art Society occupied 457 Madison.

McKim, Mead & White would lead the way out of the brownstone era to a new age marked by white limestone and marble. But on the Villard Houses they used New Jersey brownstone. The firm may not have liked the stone (Villard insisted on it), but you will never see it used better than here, where the builders took none of the shortcuts that have caused the soft stone to spall or scale from lesser structures.

21 CLUB

21 West 52nd Street
Restaurant and bar since 1929

Jack Kreindler and Charlie Berns opened a speakeasy in Greenwich Village in 1922. In 1926 they moved it to 42 West 49th Street, to a neighborhood that boasted some of the most swank speakeasies in New York. It, like many of these illicit drinking joints that had come to occupy old brownstone row houses in what had been, and was no longer, a popular residential neighborhood, was displaced by construction of the vast new Rockefeller Center. So, in 1929, Kreindler and Berns moved their establishment to just outside the northern edge of Rockefeller Center, at 21 West 52nd Street. They had previously called their speakeasy the

Puncheon Club. Now they called it the 21 Club, after their new address. As speakeasies went, 21 was no fly-by-night operation. It catered to a crowd of swells, and was cleverly outfitted with movable shelves and hidden doors for protection during police raids. The wine cellar was located via a secret passage in the house next door, at 19 West 52nd Street. After the repeal of Prohibition in 1933 (one reason the ban on alcohol was rescinded was that a desperate federal government needed the tax revenues during the Great Depression), the 21 Club made a successful transition to operating as a legitimate restaurant. It has ever since been one of the most exclusive eateries

in Manhattan, known for its devoted customer base of glittering celebrities and powerful politicians. For example, every U.S. president from Franklin Delano Roosevelt to Barack Obama (with the lone exception of George W. Bush) has dined at 21. The most distinctive feature of the building is the group of 33 painted cast-iron lawn jockeys adorning the building's front porch and stoop. These have been donated to the restaurant over the years and each lawn jockey represents a customer's stable or horse farm.

John D. Rockefeller Jr., a teetotaler none too pleased with the presence of so many speakeasies (though he would himself become an opponent of Prohibition) in his "backyard" (he lived on 54th Street between Fifth and Sixth Avenues), had chased Kreindler and Berns from 49th Street, and he nearly chased them from 52nd Street, too – but they won. If you look at a property map

you'll see that 21 is directly on the axis of the street called Rockefeller Plaza, which runs from 48th to 51st Streets. You will see that the front door of the 1939 building (erected through Rockefeller largess) of the Museum of Modern Art, on 53rd Street, is on the same axis. Rockefeller wanted to extend Rockefeller Plaza north to 53rd Street and the front door of MoMA. To do so required that he control the blocks between 51st and 53rd Streets. He had the block from the north side of 51st to the south side of 52nd, and he had the south side of 52nd. All he needed was the north side of 52nd – the 21 Club. Jack and Charlie said thanks but no thanks to Rockefeller's offer. They were happy where they were – and so were their customers. And this time, they were legal.

By the way, the old clandestine wine cellar is still the restaurant's wine cellar, and is said to be one of the finest in the city.

CENTRAL SYNAGOGUE

Lexington Avenue and 55th Street
Built 1870-72
Architect: Henry Fernbach

Central Synagogue, Congregation Ahavath Chesed, was built between 1870 and 1872 and is the oldest synagogue in continuous use in New York. The architect, Henry Fernbach (New York's first prominent Jewish architect), was inspired by the Dohány Street Synagogue (1854-59) in Budapest, Hungary, which popularized the Moorish style for synagogues. The style remembers a Jewish golden age in Medieval Spain under Muslim (Moorish) rule. Other New York synagogues in the Moorish style include Eldridge Street Synagogue (1887) at 12 Eldridge Street on the Lower East Side, and Park East Synagogue (1889-90) at 163 East 67th Street.

In 1998, a disastrous accidental fire, just as workers were completing a three-year renovation of Central Synagogue, completely collapsed the roof onto the sanctuary, turning it into a pile of rubble. The fire was so bad that at first the congregants feared their beautiful and historic house of worship was unsalvageable. Perhaps the fact that the fire spared the ark gave rise to the idea that, in fact, the building could, and would, be restored. The architects Hardy Holzman Pfeiffer took charge, and by 2001 Central Synagogue was fully restored – indeed

shone as no one had ever seen it do. The restoration was an opportunity to return the building, which had been altered and compromised through the decades, to its original glory. This is nowhere more apparent than in the extraordinary stencilwork of the sanctuary, which rings out in no fewer than sixty-nine colors. These colors had dulled over the years. Now, as when the building was brand new, the vibrant colors startle – even stun – the first-time visitor. Equally exquisite are the ornamental floor tiles – 40,000 of them. The ark is bathed in colored light that pours down from three stained-glass laylights that had been obscured for decades until the restoration uncovered them. This is one of the most exciting interiors in New York.

On the outside, the building remains an impressive structure. The facade is of contrasting bands of stone, and there is a great rose window. Twin towers are topped by vibrantly colored – gold on green – onion domes. Since this is a synagogue, the decoration is non-representational. The synagogue was built during a Victorian era fascinated by intricate abstract patterns and picturesque building profiles, and the Moorish synagogue fit right in with the spirit of the time.

CITICORP CENTER

Lexington Avenue and 53rd Street
Built 1974-77
Architects: Hugh Stubbins & Associates

Originally called Citicorp Center, this silvery 59-story tower immediately took its place among the iconic skyscrapers of Manhattan, standing tall on 114-foot-high "stilts" over a sunken plaza, and with a sloping roof – a dramatic thing after a quarter of a century of flat-topped office buildings – that made the building conspicuous on the skyline. (The roof was originally designed to slope because it was to contain solar panels. When the solar energy idea was abandoned, however, the slope was retained for purely aesthetic reasons.)

Citigroup Center rose at a time when New York had just begun to regain its swagger following a very difficult decade of financial crisis, corporate defections, rising crime, population loss, cutbacks in municipal services, and declining infrastructure. It was a symbol of hope and recovery. It also exemplified a new trend in skyscraper design. The zoning law allowed "bonus" height to buildings that incorporated public amenities. Citigroup did so in the form of a vast, multi-level atrium that contained stores, restaurants, public seating, and rest rooms; the atrium was decorated with lush plantings and offered concerts and exhibits. To some it seemed like a suburban mall, but to others it seemed inspired urbanism, a highly successful "people place" with just the right mix of attractions. Alas, following the attacks of September 11, 2001, Citigroup, one of the largest global financial conglomerates, was revealed to be the target of a thwarted bombing. The atrium, while still open to the public, is subject to tight security and no longer pulses with life as it did years ago.

In the northwest corner of the square-block site, the Citigroup tower, in an engineering tour de force, is cantilevered over St. Peter's Lutheran Church, part of the complex designed by the Boston-based Hugh Stubbins & Associates. An earlier St. Peter's on the site had sold its property to Citicorp on condition that the new complex contain a new home for the congregation. The new, granite-clad church may be the most attractive modern church in the city, with a soaring, Scandinavian-inspired sanctuary and a chapel designed by the sculptor Louise Nevelson.

LEVER HOUSE & PARK AVENUE

Park Avenue between 53rd and 54th Street
Built 1952
Architect: Gordon Bunshaft of Skidmore, Owings & Merrill

Lever House was the first glass skyscraper built in the heart of the central business district, which till then comprised only masonry-clad buildings.

Lever House thus was one of the most startling things ever built in New York. New Yorkers stopped dead in their tracks when they saw this lighter-than-air blue-green glass object hovering over stony Park Avenue. Just a few years later, of course, glass buildings had been built all over the city, and they had lost their power to

startle. So it is hard to imagine what Lever House was like when it was new.

Lever Brothers was a soap company (Dove, Lifebuoy, Irish Spring) whose chairman, Charles Luckman, was an architecture buff (who would later decide to become an architect). The new office building was designed by Gordon Bunshaft of Skidmore, Owings & Merrill.

What makes Lever House continue to impress people today is that it is so well-designed, one of the few Modernist buildings in the city built on a human scale and with real attention to human needs. A horizontal slab hovers over the west side of Park Avenue from 52nd to 53rd Streets, with a broad, hollowed-out pedestrian plaza on its south end. A vertical slab tower rises from the northern edge of the horizontal base; the tower's narrow end faces Park Avenue, so that the "front" of the tower is visible from blocks away. So little of the "zoning envelope" was used that the building seemed almost a benefaction to the people of New York.

It is said that one reason Lever was eager for an all-glass building was that, by being constantly cleaned, it would gleam, and in so doing make people think of soap.

SONY BUILDING

Madison Avenue between 55th and 56th Streets
Built 1984
Architects: Philip Johnson and John Burgee

When Philip Johnson and John Burgee's AT&T Building opened in 1984, it was the most talked-about and debated building in the world. Since rechristened the Sony Building, the 37-story tower is now pretty much taken for granted. The revolution of which it seemed the harbinger never really played out as some thought it would.

That revolution was called "Post-Modernism." From the end of World War II to the 1980s, American architecture was dominated by the Modernist aesthetic that had originated in central Europe in the years following the First World War. As applied to downtown office buildings, it meant the "glass box vernacular" that flowed from such works as Mies van der Rohe's Seagram Building (1958). One after another the tall office buildings went up following a cookie-cutter approach, and by the 1980s not just the public but architects had grown bored, and wanted something more. Mies van der Rohe had said "Less is more"; Post-Modernist Robert Venturi said "Less is a bore."

Philip Johnson had worked on the Seagram Building and as the onetime curator of architecture at the Museum of Modern Art had been a vociferous advocate of Modernism. Now he turned his back on the glass box and designed a granite-clad building with a high-arched entryway and a shocking top with a classical broken pediment modeled on a Chippendale high-boy dresser. The building was featured on the cover of *Time* magazine and people came to New York to see it. But Post-Modernism failed to sustain the momentum. This was in part due to the limitations their educations had placed on modern architects, who were not trained in the traditional skills that would enable them to incorporate classical forms in their work without looking like they were mocking those forms.

AT&T had included a pedestrian arcade at the building's base in exchange for the right to make the tower higher than the zoning would otherwise permit. When Sony took over the building in 1992, the company received permission to enclose the open space and use it as a products showroom.

The Sony Building and the adjacent IBM Building (1983, Edward Larrabee Barnes & Associates, architects) and Trump Tower were all built around the same time, occasioning a now-forgotten flurry of articles and op-ed pieces voicing concern over the "overbuilding" of Manhattan – concerns that from the standpoint of a quarter century later seem quaint.

PALEY PARK

3 East 53rd Street
Built 1967
Landscape architects: Zion & Breen

Paley Park, on 53rd Street just east of Fifth Avenue, in the midst of one of the most congested and frenetic parts of midtown Manhattan, proved that the tiniest park, designed right and put in the right place, could have an impact as great as that of a park twenty times its size. At less than an acre (0.96 acres to be precise, or 4200 square feet), Paley Park is small indeed. What makes this tiny park, which opened in 1967, so great? It occupies a single building lot, cradled between two buildings, which, with the rear of a building on 54th Street, tightly define the space, turning it into what architects like to call an "urban room." A 20-foot-high "waterwall" creates a dramatic backdrop. In this compact space, the sound of the water (1800 gallons a minute) actually blocks out the city noises that, at 53rd Street and Fifth Avenue, are pretty intense. The side walls are covered in ivy, there are several well-spaced shady locust trees, and there are a few potted plants. These plantings are crucial to the success here, but do note that they are not overwhelming in number. The park (or parklet) is also set off from its surroundings by being ever so slightly raised: The park's pavement is four steps above the sidewalk of 53rd Street. There is a food stand where park users can buy a sandwich or a cup of coffee – because who does not like to nibble or sip when relaxing in a park? Yet such stands were rare in public space design

at the time. And then the finishing touch: movable chairs and tables. Such a simple thing is often the difference between an extremely successful public space (as here), and one that is completely dead (such as Grace Plaza, at the southeast corner of the Avenue of the Americas and 43rd Street). Park users want the freedom to move their chairs into groups, to move them into privacy (perhaps away from that leering man), to move them into and out of the sun (so important!), and at Paley Park they can. His minute observation of how people actually use Paley Park led famed urbanist William H. Whyte to champion many of its elements in other public space-design projects, notably in his role as a consultant in the 1990s redesign of Bryant Park on the Avenue of the Americas between 40th and 42nd Streets. The same concepts can be seen in almost every public

space project in the city since the 1990s.

The site on which Paley Park was built was occupied from 1929 to 1965 by one of New York's most legendary nightspots, the Stork Club. Owned by Sherman Billingsley, for more than three decades the Stork Club was home to "café society," which included a mix of socialites and media celebrities. Frank Sinatra, Marilyn Monroe, and various Kennedys were regulars. When it closed, William S. Paley, the media executive who built the Columbia Broadcasting Service (CBS), created Paley Park through his eponymous foundation. To this day, Paley Park is privately owned, but open to the public. The Project for Public Spaces, a highly respected watchdog and advocacy group concerned with the design of public spaces, has placed Paley Park – all 0.96 acres of it – on its list of the World's Best Parks.

MoMA

53rd Street between Fifth and Sixth Avenues
Built 1939
Architects: Philip L. Goodwin (1885-1958) and Edward Durell Stone (1902-1978)
Architect of 2004 renovation: Yoshio Taniguchi (born 1937)

The Museum of Modern Art, or MoMA as New Yorkers call it, was founded by three remarkable New York ladies, Abby Aldrich Rockefeller, Lillie Bliss, and Mary Sullivan. Each was an art collector, and they met making the rounds of galleries. As they got to know one another and shared their passion for modern art, they eventually hatched the idea of MoMA. They hired a brilliant, virtually unknown young curator, Alfred Barr, and the museum was founded in 1929 in the Crown Building on Fifth Avenue and 57th Street. When MoMA outgrew its space in that building, Abby and her husband, John D. Rockefeller Jr., donated land, including eventually their own house, on 53rd and 54th Streets between Fifth and Sixth Avenues. Edward Durell Stone, who had helped design Radio City Music Hall, and Philip Goodwin, a member of MoMA's board and an architect known for traditional country houses, designed the eye-popping, marble-and-glass modern building that opened on 53rd Street in 1939. Back then, the pearly white museum was like a shaft of sunlight on a dour, all-brownstone street. In the years just after World War II, MoMA had as great an international prestige as any arts institution in the world.

In the 1980s, in part better to handle blockbusters like the monumental Picasso retrospective of 1980, MoMA undertook a major expansion project designed by Cesar Pelli & Associates. This included construction of the adjacent apartment skyscraper called

Museum Tower. But it wasn't enough, and in fewer than twenty years MoMA expanded again. This time the Japanese minimalist architect Yoshio Taniguchi was in charge, creating new airy, whitewashed galleries.

MoMA has always been famous for going beyond fine art as traditionally defined, and was one of the first museums to boast departments of architecture, industrial design, film, and photography.

For many New Yorkers, the most delectable part of MoMA is its Sculpture Garden on 54th Street, on the site of the Rockefellers' town house. Designed by Philip Johnson (who was MoMA's original curator of architecture) and opened in 1953, the garden was minimally redesigned in 2004 by Taniguchi. It is one of the superb spots for people-watching in New York.

Among the masterpieces of modern painting to be seen in MoMA are Vincent Van Gogh's 'The Starry Night' (1889), Pablo Picasso's 'Les Demoiselles d'Avignon' (1907), and 'Flag' (1954-55) by Jasper Johns.

TIFFANY & CO.

Fifth Avenue and 57th Street
Built 1940
Architects: Cross & Cross

Who can think of Tiffany's without recalling the 1961 film *Breakfast at Tiffany's*? But think for a moment of Tiffany's before Audrey Hepburn. For this is one of the oldest retail businesses operating in New York City. Charles Lewis Tiffany and his partner John B. Young founded the firm in 1837, making it almost as old as Brooks Brothers (1818), and Lord & Taylor (1826). That same year they settled on "Tiffany blue" as the firm's signature color, still in use today. Tiffany's started out at 259 Broadway, near City Hall, before moving to 550 Broadway, where the iconic "Atlas clock" was first installed over the store's entrance. This is also where Tiffany's was located during the Civil War, when the firm designed and manufactured medals, epaulets, swords and scabbards, insignia, and more for the Union Army. Tiffany's moved to Fifth Avenue and 57th Street in 1940, to a streamlined Art Moderne building designed by Cross & Cross – it was the first air-conditioned retail store in the world. Holly Golightly says in *Breakfast at Tiffany's* that whenever she gets a case of the "mean reds," she goes straight to Tiffany's: "Calms me down right away. The quietness and the proud look of it; nothing very bad could happen to you there."

TRUMP TOWER

Fifth Avenue and 56th Street
Built 1983
Architects: Swanke Hayden Connell

The Tiffany store shares the east side of Fifth Avenue between 56th and 57th Streets with another, but much younger, Manhattan landmark, Trump Tower. The sleek, 58-story, faceted black-glass tower was designed by Swanke Hayden Connell and opened in 1983. It is known for its dramatic atrium, which features five levels of shopping, a large "waterwall," walls of pink marble, and lots of brass and mirrors. People stream through the space all day long. The Trump atrium connects with that of the IBM Building at the northwest corner of Madison Avenue and 56th Street, and to the Niketown store, located at 6 East 57th Street in a space that, from 1991 to 1995, housed an ill-fated branch of the famous Paris department store Galeries Lafayette.

THE ED KOCH QUEENSBORO BRIDGE

Manhattan entrance to pedestrian walkway Second Avenue and 59th Street
Opened 1909
Engineer: Gustav Lindenthal
Architect: Henry Hornbostel

The Queensboro Bridge opened on March 30, 1909, connecting Manhattan's 59th Street with Queens Boulevard across the river. (Simon & Garfunkel's 1966 song "59th Street Bridge Song [Feelin' Groovy]" refers to it.) It was the third bridge to connect Manhattan to Long Island. Brooklyn Bridge (1883) and the Williamsburg Bridge (1903) were both suspension bridges, slung majestically across the river in single spans seemingly defiant of physical law. The Queensboro is different. It's a cantilever bridge, touching down for support about halfway across the river, on Roosevelt Island. Yet, while lacking the swooping splendor of its predecessors, the Queensboro is just as beautiful. Note Hornbostel's delightful aesthetic touches: wonderful finials atop the 350-foot-high towers make the bridge seem to skip across the water in a manner as pleasing as the effervescent glide of the suspension spans. The great stone piers are like a sequence of triumphal arches supporting the bridge's lyrically curving steel superstructure.

In 1979, the Koch administration opened the bicycle and pedestrian lane. However, bridge reconstruction projects in the '80s and '90s meant it was not until 1999 that a permanent "People's Roadway" began operation. In 2011, the bridge was officially

renamed the Ed Koch Queensboro Bridge, in honor of New York City's mayor from 1978 to 1989.

From the 1910s to the 1930s there was a wholesale food market on the Manhattan end of the bridge. In the 1990s, the new Bridgemarket – comprising a restaurant, a supermarket, a Conran shop, and a public plaza – opened inside and outside the remarkable market halls built into the bridge. The soaring spaces have ceilings of self-supporting Guastavino tiles, which can be seen in the supermarket at the west end. Also look for the beautiful Evangeline Blashfield Memorial, outside in the plaza, by Edwin Howland Blashfield, America's greatest mural painter. Here he created a mural of mosaic glass tiles showing a languorously elegant woman resting her left elbow upon a cornucopia spilling its fruits – a riot of purples, oranges, blues, reds, and yellows. It's truly one of the loveliest unexpected things in Manhattan.

PLAZA HOTEL & PULITZER FOUNTAIN

Fifth Avenue between 58th and 59th Streets
Built 1907
Architect: Henry Janeway Hardenbergh (1847-1918)

The Plaza Hotel is a New York icon – as recognizable a landmark as the Brooklyn Bridge – and a place invested by New Yorkers with many memories, of afternoon tea in the Palm Court, weddings in the Grand Ballroom, corporate conferences, and college mixers. Opened in 1907, the Plaza was designed in a modified French Renaissance style by Henry J. Hardenbergh. He had earlier (1880-84) designed the famed Dakota Apartments on Central Park West and 72nd Street. At first it seems the two buildings are very different: the Dakota dark and Victorian, the Plaza bright and white and very much of the "City Beautiful" era. But close inspection reveals the buildings to have similar châteauesque profiles and details. Still, the Plaza is the more glittering building, its white brick and limestone mass, rising majestically behind the open space of Grand Army Plaza, reflecting back the sunlight that showers the building, making it gleam and glisten by day. This effect is accentuated by the lovely Pulitzer Fountain, erected in 1916 and designed by Thomas Hastings, in front of the hotel. The Plaza was expanded and enhanced in 1919-21 by Warren & Wetmore, architects of Grand Central Terminal. They added the elegantly canopied Fifth Avenue entrance, as well as several important interior spaces. But the building is mostly Hardenbergh's. Inside, the Palm Court is especially noteworthy, with its spectacular stained-glass laylight, recently restored. All Americans of a certain age also know the Plaza for six-and-a-half-year-old Eloise. In

1955, Kay Thompson, an outstanding nightclub chanteuse who frequently performed at the Plaza's Persian Room, wrote a children's book, illustrated by Hilary Knight, about the adventures of a frolicsome girl who lives in the Plaza Hotel. The book and its sequels made the Plaza for many years the most famous building in New York among America's children. Look for Hilary Knight's 1964 oil portrait of Eloise, which hangs in the corridor along the south side of the Palm Court.

APPLE STORE

767 Fifth Avenue at 58th Street
Built 2006
Architects: Bohlin Cywinski Jackson

Apple products – from the *iMac* and *MacBook Pro* to the *iPhone* and *iPad* – are known for their superior modern design. The Cupertino, California-based company, founded in 1976 by Steve Jobs and Steve Wozniak, operates more than 300 retail stores worldwide, and each of these must exhibit the same degree of thoughtful, sleek design as the company's products. Many of the stores are located in already existing buildings, such as the Apple Store at 401 West 14th Street, located in a converted market building from 1923, and the Apple Store at 103 Prince Street, in a converted post office from 1909.

However, the Apple Store on Fifth Avenue, between 58th and 59th Streets, right across the avenue from the Plaza Hotel, is a new building, built in 2006, and as such had to be as good an example of Apple design as the *iPod Nano*. The architects Bohlin Cywinski Jackson, designers of many Apple Stores, responded with the remarkable glass cube that adorns the once problematic plaza of the former General Motors Building (1968, Edward Durell Stone). The plaza was originally sunken – one could enter it and access its shops only by descending stairs. Almost all the sunken plazas that were briefly fashionable in the 1960s and 1970s have failed as public places. (The Rockefeller Center's sunken plaza (see page 118), from the 1930s, was saved only by being converted to an ice-skating rink.) When real estate mogul Donald Trump took control of the building, he wisely rebuilt the plaza at ground level. Later, the Apple cube was built. The glass cube hovers over a stairway that leads down into the store. If people once were reluctant to climb down into the General Motors plaza, they have no such reluctance when it comes to the Apple Store, which is typically one of the most crowded places in Manhattan, and is open twenty-four hours a day. In 2009, a study done at Cornell University found that the Fifth Avenue Apple Store was the fifth most photographed building in New York on Flickr.

Intriguingly, Peter Bohlin, who founded his architectural firm in Wilkes-Barre, Pennsylvania, in 1965, is not only Apple's architect, but also designed the spectacular 66,000-square-foot mansion of Apple's arch-rival, Bill Gates, in Medina, Washington. Even more remarkably, given his client roster, Bohlin claims he is completely computer-illiterate, and does not even use email, let alone CAD.

CENTRAL PARK & BETHESDA FOUNTAIN

Fifth Avenue to Central Park West, 59th to 110th Streets
Built 1850s-1870s
Landscape architects: Calvert Vaux and Frederick Law Olmsted

Central Park is one of the greatest American works of art of the 19th century. It may at first sound a little strange to call it a work of art. A work of art you can play softball in? Isn't it a nature preserve in the middle of Manhattan? In fact, Central Park was designed and built, down to the ripples in the earth. It is not at all what this part of Manhattan looked like in its natural state. Indeed, nothing in its natural state looks like Central Park, because the park's visionary designers compacted and juxtaposed landscapes in a way never found in nature. They were, however, very much trying to create an experience of nature for the people of the city.

New York in the 1830s and 1840s was one of the fastest-growing cities on earth. Immigrants poured in from Ireland and Germany, swelling not just the city's population but the population of the city's poor. Vast slums emerged. The 1840s saw the first purpose-built multiple-unit dwellings, called tenements, soon built in the thousands to house – to warehouse – the city's poor. Not only was life in the slums nearly unendurable for their inhabitants, but better-off New Yorkers feared the growing social tensions arising from the growing poverty and the gulf between rich and poor. The city was crowded, dirty, malodorous, dangerous, and tense, and a hotbed of infectious diseases. As concerned New Yorkers looked around for solutions, some thought the city's problems to be endemic to cities themselves, and that the best way to solve the problems of city life was to make the city a little less city-like. The poet and newspaper editor William Cullen Bryant and the extremely influential landscape gardener Andrew Jackson Downing led the charge by calling upon the city to create a large park – like none that had ever been built or even dreamed of in America – that would allow city dwellers to get out of the city without, well, getting out of the city. Such a park would provide a perfect experience of nature, of meadows and forests and hills and trees and birds. It would be a peaceful oasis where the

slum dweller could breathe clean air, and where all New Yorkers, rich and poor, would be perfect equals in their enjoyment and contemplation of nature.

The city acquired most of the land for the park in 1853, and hired a journalist and itinerant gentleman farmer named Frederick Law Olmsted to supervise the clearing of the land bounded by 59th Street on the south, 106th Street on the north (later extended to 110th), Fifth Avenue on the east, and Eighth Avenue (later called Central Park West) on the west. It was rocky, swampy, generally unprepossessing land. Some of it was occupied: An African-American settlement called Seneca Village and a Roman Catholic convent were among the properties displaced by "eminent domain." In 1858 a competition was held for the design. Downing, a gifted landscape gardener, would likely have been selected to design the park had he not died in a tragic steamboat accident. His assistant, an English architect named Calvert Vaux, created a spectacular design, and to improve his chances of winning the commission prevailed upon Olmsted, who had extensive knowledge of the land and of the politics involved, to join him in a partnership. The strategy worked and they began almost immediately on the realization of their visionary design.

Central Park is much too vast a story to go into here. The park is designed in the romantic tradition, drawing on English sources, and includes very few straight lines. It's designed with lots of curves, and ever-shifting vistas that

provide continual surprise and delight to the park visitor. It also brings into close proximity pastoral countryside and sublime wilderness. The park, though, does have a straight spine: the Mall, located in the southeastern quadrant roughly from the line of 66th Street to that of 72nd Street. The great 19th-century New York diarist George Templeton Strong called this the one "Versailles-y" part of the park. The Mall is a beautiful avenue under a roof of arcing American elms (the finest stand of these trees remaining in New York State). It is like the nave of a cathedral. The Mall

was created to provide parkgoers a way of orienting themselves – and to allow rich New Yorkers a place to parade their gorgeous carriages. One walks along the Mall, past statues of literary worthies (Shakespeare, Robert Burns, Walter Scott, Fitz-Greene Halleck), to an amazing structure, Bethesda Terrace, special not least because it was created for no purpose other than to provide delight. One can walk down a flight of stairs under the terrace, or around the sides and down stairs, to arrive at a broad plaza fronting Central Park's Lake. In the center of the plaza is Emma Stebbins's

beautiful statue of the Angel of the Waters: the angel stirs the water, thus purifying it – it is a reference to New York's Croton water system. The sandstone terrace is magnificently carved in the most dazzling panoply of images – fruits and flowers and birds – to be seen in New York. The decoration was designed by Vaux's assistant and fellow Englishman Jacob Wrey Mould, and carved by hand by skilled artisans, including recent German immigrants. On the ceiling of the inside portion of the terrace are spectacularly colored tiles, designed by Mould and manufactured by Minton in England. On the other side of the Lake from here is the thickly wooded part of the park called the Ramble. Nowhere in New York, perhaps in America, do architecture, art, and nature come together to create something so right and so beautiful as here.

Be aware, also, that since 1980 Central Park has undergone a monumental restoration under the public-private Central Park Conservancy. The park had been in awful shape. Today it's fashionable to say it looks as good as at any time since its opening. Actually, it looks better.

HEARST TOWER

Eighth Avenue between 56th and 57th Streets
Built 2006
Architect: Foster + Partners

Press baron William Randolph Hearst, the model for Orson Welles's *Citizen Kane*, built what is today the lower, masonry part of this building in 1928 to house the offices of his magazine empire, which included at the time *Good Housekeeping* (yes, there is a Good Housekeeping Institute, and it is in this building), *Cosmopolitan*, and *Harper's Bazaar*. The Hearst Corporation later added such titles as *Esquire*, *Redbook*, *Seventeen*, and *Woman's Day*. Hearst's architect was Joseph Urban, known more as a set designer, especially for the Ziegfeld Follies, and nightclub designer (the Persian Room in the Plaza Hotel, the Central Park Casino) than as a designer of buildings. But Urban was a versatile designer, and all his works exhibited great flair. Urban's 1928 building was conceived as the base for a tower, but the tower was put on indefinite hold, and not until 2006 was it finally realized.

Of course, the eventual tower bears very little relation to the original building. British architect Norman Foster's great 46-story faceted, diamond-patterned glass tower rises from within the walls of the older building. The final product baffles some New Yorkers, and excites others. Some people like new buildings to be designed in continuity with the old, others enjoy the clash of styles. One need not travel far to see Cesar Pelli's Carnegie Hall Tower, on 57th Street between Sixth and Seventh Avenues. The Pelli tower, built in 1991, rises over historic Carnegie Hall, and tries hard to strike a note of continuity. You will decide for yourself which approach you prefer.

The older Hearst Building remains only as a shell. It was completely gutted when the new tower was built, and much of its interior is now the dramatic lobby of the tower, featuring steep escalators across a vast "waterwall" leading to the building's elevator banks.

Norman Foster, Baron Foster of Thames Bank, was the 1999 recipient of the prestigious Pritzker Architecture Prize, and is the architect of some of the world's most famous buildings, such as the HSBC Headquarters in Hong Kong. He is also the architect of the 79-story Two World Trade Center, which has a projected completion date of 2020.

COLUMBUS CIRCLE: TIME WARNER CENTER, MUSEUM OF ARTS & DESIGN

Broadway between 58th and 60th Streets, west side of Columbus Circle
Built 2000-2003
Architect: David Childs of Skidmore, Owings & Merrill

Time Warner Center rose on a magnificently located but perennially troubled site on the west side of Columbus Circle. For many years the site was occupied by the New York Coliseum, built by master planner Robert Moses to serve as the city's principal convention center. After the larger Jacob K. Javits Center was built in the West 30s near the Hudson River, the Coliseum became obsolete. The city, which owned the building, sought to realize a substantial windfall by selling the site to the highest bidder in the midst of a red-hot real-estate market. In the 1980s, a massive project called Columbus Center, designed by the innovative Israeli architect Moshe Safdie, was proposed. But concerned citizens, led by the civic organization the Municipal Art Society, brought suit against the city to stop the project. Critics claimed that the city had allowed an illegal zoning variance and that the scale of the project threatened to place much of neighboring Central Park in perpetual shadow.

The present Time Warner Center, opened in 2003, is the replacement project. Designed by David Childs of Skidmore, Owings & Merrill, the sleek, glass-clad twin 55-story towers can look from some angles as thin as knife blades. In the center's stone- and glass-faced base is a large multi-level shopping mall, famous for its several fine restaurants,

among them Thomas Keller's Per Se, considered one of the best restaurants in the world. In the lower level is a vast Whole Foods Market, while another section of the base is given over to an outpost of nearby Lincoln Center for the Performing Arts. Under the direction of famed trumpeter Wynton Marsalis, Jazz at Lincoln Center features several performing venues. The center also features the luxury Mandarin Oriental Hotel, offices (including, of course, those of Time Warner), and some of the most expensive condominium apartments in New York.

Even those not in love with the architecture must concede that the center has brought life to a place that had been lifeless for half a century or more. The old Coliseum was a scaleless building with big blank walls, making for a dreary streetscape that pedestrians tried their hardest to avoid. Today the area pulses with life.

A superb rostral column – an ancient Roman form in which a defeated navy's prows and anchors are embedded in a commemorative column – topped by a statue of Christopher Columbus marks the center of the circle; designed by Gaetano Russo and dedicated in 1892, the column has been restored and provided with a new landscaped setting. On the south side of the circle stands the Museum of Arts and Design, which opened on the site in 2008. The

building, by Brad Cloepfil and Allied Works Architecture, is actually a comprehensive remodeling of the earlier 2 Columbus Circle, designed by Edward Durell Stone and built in 1964.

On the north side of the circle is the Trump International Hotel & Tower, a 1997 reconstruction by architects Philip Johnson and Alan Ritchie of the 1969 Gulf and Western Building.

LINCOLN CENTER FOR THE PERFORMING ARTS

60th to 66th Streets, Columbus to Amsterdam Avenues
Philharmonic Hall opened 1962, New York State Theater opened 1964,
Metropolitan Opera House opened 1966
Architects: Wallace K. Harrison (master plan and Metropolitan Opera House),
Max Abramovitz (Philharmonic Hall), Philip Johnson and
John Burgee (plaza and New York State Theater)

Lincoln Square was a working-class neighborhood of tenements and mom-and-pop shops. This was the West Side referred to in the title of *West Side Story*. The poverty and substandard housing made the area ripe for "urban renewal." In the 1950s and 1960s the government condemned whole neighborhoods, bulldozed them, and replaced them with new developments. Usually the new developments were of high-rise apartments, and the Lincoln Square urban renewal project included the vast Lincoln Towers development. (The Towers replaced old tenements that, between their condemnation and demolition, served as sets for the 1961 film version of *West Side Story*.) But the renewal project's focus was the cultural complex called Lincoln Center for the Performing Arts. Although the project as a whole was guided by Robert Moses, New York's master planner from the 1930s to the 1960s, the lead in shaping Lincoln Center came from John D. Rockefeller III. Since World War II, New

York had become what it had never before been: the culture capital of the world. In the Cold War years, Rockefeller wanted New York – and America – to be able to present to the world in a single, unforgettable image that this was the new reality. Look at Lincoln Center, and you'd know instantly of America's unparalleled cultural assets.

Those assets included the New York Philharmonic, which performed in Philharmonic (now Avery Fisher) Hall, opened in 1962 on the north side of the Philip Johnson-designed plaza; the New York City Ballet, which performed in the New York State Theater, opened in 1964 on the south side of the plaza; and the Metropolitan Opera Company, which performed in the Metropolitan

Opera House, opened in 1966 on the west side of the plaza. The plaza and these three buildings are what everyone thinks of when they think of Lincoln Center. The Met used to perform in an 1883 building on Broadway and 39th Street. The company got its long-awaited new home in the form of Wallace K. Harrison's travertine-clad, mock-classical edifice with its five great arches rising with a certain majesty behind the plaza's central fountain. It opened on September 16, 1966, with a production of Samuel Barber's *Antony and Cleopatra* starring Leontyne Price and Justino Diaz. Among the celebrities in the audience were Mrs. Lyndon B. Johnson, then the First Lady, seated in her box with Ferdinand and Imelda Marcos.

THE DAKOTA

Central Park West and West 72nd Street
Built 1880-84
Architect: Henry J. Hardenbergh

The development of the Upper West Side of Manhattan had a troubled gestation. It was originally intended to be a planned district – New York's answer to Haussmann's Paris. But municipal corruption scandals – involving the downfall of "Boss" Tweed – followed by a devastating national depression put the area to the west of the celebrated new Central Park in a state of suspended animation: roads partly cut through, parks partly built, the whole dotted by the shantytowns of those made indigent by the economic meltdown. Not till the elevated railroad – the city's first form of rapid mass transportation – opened along Ninth (Columbus) Avenue around 1880 did the area's prospects perk up, with Edward Clark, the rich and powerful president of the Singer Sewing Machine Company, taking the informal lead among a group of speculative developers, and in so doing becoming the *de facto* master planner of the new district.

Clark's vision included a neighborhood comprising both row houses and apartment houses. The latter had only lately come on the scene. Well-to-do New Yorkers had always insisted upon private homes. Only the poor lived in multiple-unit dwellings, which were called tenements. But after the Civil War, rising land values and changing lifestyles slowly, but surely, pushed the middle class, followed by the upper class, into the new apartment buildings, the first of which were built in areas of the city that had already undergone development. The Upper West Side, under Clark's tutelage, would be the first urban neighborhood in America developed from its inception to include apartment buildings.

One of these, the most famous, was built by Clark, who named it the Dakota. The old saw is that the building seemed so remote from the business centers that it might as well be, said some, in the Dakota Territory. In fact, the building was built where it was because the new elevated trains placed it within minutes of the business centers. Clark probably was just indulging a patriotic urge in his suggestion that buildings and streets of the new neighborhood be named for the nation's latest additions and annexations.

Designed by Henry J. Hardenbergh in a French château style, though in a somber Victorian palette, the building offered luxurious living on the edge of Central Park. A charming story has the composer Tchaikovsky visiting New York and staying in the Dakota apartment of music publisher Gustav Schirmer. Tchaikovsky did not at first realize that the entire building was not Schirmer's mansion – and Central Park

the mansion's grounds!

On a much more somber note, the Dakota was the scene of the murder of John Lennon on the night of December 8, 1980. Lennon and his wife, Yoko Ono,

had lived in the Dakota since 1973. Lennon was shot and killed by Mark David Chapman just outside the vaulted entryway that leads from West 72nd Street to the Dakota's large internal courtyard. In 1985, Strawberry Fields, a two-and-a-half-acre memorial to Lennon, was dedicated at the western edge of Central Park, directly across the street from the Dakota.

THE ANSONIA HOTEL

Broadway between 73rd and 74th Streets
Built 1899-1904
Architects: Paul Emile Duboy and William E.D. Stokes

William Earl Dodge Stokes, scion of old money (the Phelps-Dodge mining fortune), was the eccentric builder of the Ansonia Hotel. He closely oversaw the building's design by Paul Emile Duboy (1857-1907), a rare French architect working in New York at the time. The extraordinary profusion of ornamentation provided Parisian grandeur, but at a scale that was all-American: If the Ansonia had been built in Paris, it would have been by far that city's tallest building. As it was, the Ansonia ranked with a handful of other Broadway buildings erected to coincide with the opening of the very first line of the Interborough Rapid Transit Company subway as the largest apartment houses that had ever been built. The Ansonia's plumbing contract is said to be the largest in history up to that time.

Stokes was obsessed with making the building fireproof. To that end he insulated the apartments in foot-thick terra-cotta partitions that would break the spread of flames. But those partitions also made the apartments soundproof – a boon to musicians. Over the years the building's tenants have included Arturo Toscanini, Igor Stravinsky, Enrico Caruso, Geraldine Farrar, Feodor Chaliapin, Lily Pons, Yehudi Menuhin, and other musical luminaries, as well as Broadway impresario Florenz Ziegfeld, baseball

star Babe Ruth, and heavyweight boxing champion Jack Dempsey. The Ansonia, in its leaner years following World War II, serves as the setting of Saul Bellow's famous novella *Seize the Day*.

Stokes kept a farm on the building's roof. There he raised goats, whose milk he liked to drink, and chickens, whose eggs he sold to the building's tenants. Once married to Rita de Acosta (later Rita Lydig), called the most beautiful woman in the world by the famous portrait painter Paul Helleu, Stokes had a reputation as a playboy. On one occasion he was shot by two chorus girls, and it was a measure of Stokes's reputation that the courts acquitted

the shooters, who claimed Stokes had harassed them.

The Ansonia was an "apartment hotel" where the residents were, for the most part, long term, though they received hotel-like housekeeping services. Meals, for example, could be taken in-room, served from a central kitchen, or eaten in the building's restaurant. From 1968 to 1975 the Continental Baths, a legendary gay bathhouse, complete with disco, and cabaret lounge, operated in what had originally been the Ansonia's basement steam baths. It was at the Continental that singers Bette Midler and Barry Manilow first rose to stardom.

AMERICAN MUSEUM OF NATURAL HISTORY

Central Park West between 77th and 81st Streets
Built mainly between 1874 and 1934
Architect of 77th Street facade: J.C. Cady & Co.
Architect of Theodore Roosevelt Memorial wing: John Russell Pope

The American Museum of Natural History was founded in 1869 at a time when our understanding of the natural world, and man's place in it, was undergoing a profound change. Meanwhile, the commissioners of Central Park, which was still under construction at that time, were also in charge of planning a new neighborhood in the sparsely settled land to the west of the park.

Along 77th Street the 700-foot-long facade, built mainly in the 1890s, was designed by Josiah Cleaveland Cady in the rugged late 19th-century style called "Richardsonian Romanesque." (Architect H.H. Richardson had adapted the Medieval Romanesque architecture of southern France and Spain into something that, in its use of rough masonry, deep window reveals, and bold massing seemed like a Medieval fortress, with grace notes of delicate terra-cotta ornamentation, and in the end became a national American style of architecture. Richardson did not design this museum, but his acolytes were everywhere in the 1880s and 1890s.) Cady's pinkish-brown sandstone and granite facade is one of the most impressive structures in Manhattan.

Turn the corner onto Central Park West and you see something startlingly different, a grand classical composition in white limestone, with a high colonnade. This front dates from 1931-34 and was designed by John Russell Pope, architect of the National Gallery of Art and the Jefferson

Memorial in Washington, D.C. Pope's part of the museum is known as the Theodore Roosevelt Memorial wing, honoring the native New Yorker who became the 26th president of the United States. Set into the grand staircase is an equestrian statue of Roosevelt, by the sculptor James Earle Fraser, who was a friend of Roosevelt and the designer in 1913 of the famous buffalo nickel.

The museum boasts some of the most awesome collections and exhibits in the world, including the 28 diroamas of the Akeley Hall of African Mammals; the Hall of Human Origins, with dioramas and other exhibits explaining evolution; gems and minerals (including the Star of India sapphire); dinosaur skeletons made of real fossils, and much, much more.

ROSE CENTER FOR EARTH AND SPACE

81st Street between Central Park West and Columbus Avenue
Built 2000
Architect: The Polshek Partnership

Many New Yorkers mourned the the old Hayden Planetarium when it was demolished in 1997. That 1935 structure, appended to the north side of the almost inconceivably vast American Museum of Natural History, had long ceased being the state-of-the-art planetarium it had been back during the Great Depression, but New Yorkers can be very sentimental about the buildings they grew up with, and in 1997 many a New Yorker could fondly recall school or family trips to the quaint old planetarium. But the museum decided that it again wanted the world's most advanced planetarium, and the old facility could not be retrofitted to make it so. So down it went, replaced by a building that New Yorkers themselves found to their great surprise was an instant classic. Designed by the Polshek Partnership, the new planetarium – still called the Hayden Planetarium – is housed within a giant sphere that appears to float within a great glass cube.

It opened in 2000. The whole thing is called the Frederick Phineas and Sandra Priest Rose Center for Earth and Space. (These are the same Roses who funded the magnificent renovation of the New York Public Library's Rose Main Reading Room.) When it opened, this was the most advanced planetarium in the world, making use of the latest in computer technology and of space imaging, including that provided by the Hubble telescope – not to mention the narrating voices of Tom Hanks and Jodie Foster. Overall, for anyone wanting to learn about the universe – from the Big Bang, to black holes – there is nothing else in America like the Rose Center. Adding to its popularity and prestige is its director, the astrophysicist Neil deGrasse Tyson, regarded by many as the best communicator of advanced scientific ideas to the public since Carl Sagan. For all its futuristic, high-tech look, the Rose Center has roots in 18th-century French architecture: The floating sphere was inspired by Étienne-Louis Boullée's proposed cenotaph honoring Isaac Newton, from 1784.

THE FRICK COLLECTION

Fifth Avenue and 70th Street
House completed 1914, converted to museum 1935
Architects: Carrère & Hastings

Henry Clay Frick (1849-1919), a force in the steel industry, commissioned Carrère & Hastings, architects of the New York Public Library, to design his palatial house on Fifth Avenue between 70th and 71st Streets, complete with that extreme rarity in Manhattan, a front lawn. The limestone house, French classical in style, is one of the finest ever built in New York. It was designed to house not only Frick, his wife Adelaide, and their daughter Helen, but also Frick's spectacular collection of fine and decorative arts. Indeed, object by object there was not a private collection of greater quality anywhere. The house was completed in 1914. Frick intended that upon his and his wife's deaths, the house and its contents would be transformed into a public museum. This happened in 1935, when John Russell Pope, architect of the National Gallery of Art in Washington, D.C., and of the Theodore Roosevelt Memorial wing of the American Museum of Natural History on Central Park West, repurposed the house as a museum.

Today it is among that handful of absolute must-see attractions in New York. The stunning, richly appointed rooms, filled with magnificent furniture and porcelain, sculpture and paintings, completely belie the notion that art is best experienced in minimalist spaces with whitewashed walls. Here, everything enhances everything else, the rich wall moldings

(as fine as any in New York) working to show off, not compete with, the art. It is all pure genius. And the art on display is almost overwhelming in that almost everything here is a masterpiece. Some paintings – Giovanni Bellini's *St. Francis in the Desert*, Hans Holbein's portrait of *Sir Thomas More*, Rembrandt's *The Polish Rider* (as well as one of Rembrandt's most moving self-portraits), Johannes Vermeer's *Mistress and Maid* – rank among the very greatest paintings to be found in America. A whole room is devoted to the series of paintings called *The Progress of Love* by Jean-Honoré Fragonard, the greatest French painter

of the 18th century. These paintings were once owned by J.P. Morgan, who hung them in the dining room of his South Kensington town house in London. Morgan died in 1913. Between 1914 and 1916 the Metropolitan Museum of Art, of which Morgan had been president, exhibited some 4,100 items from Morgan's collection, including *The Progress of Love*, hung in a replica of the London dining room. But the Met did not get to keep the paintings. Joseph Duveen, adviser to both Morgan's son, Jack, and to Frick, brokered the 1915 sale of the paintings, for $1.25 million, to Frick.

Before the Frick mansion was built, the site was occupied by a famous building: the Lenox Library. This was a private library open to the public. When the New York Public Library was founded in the 1890s, its initial purpose was to merge two great private libraries, the Astor Library and the Lenox Library. Before Frick could begin building his house, he had to wait for the completion of the New York Public Library's building on Fifth Avenue and 42nd Street, for only then could the books be removed from the Lenox Library and the building be torn down. The Lenox Library had been designed by Richard Morris Hunt, a figure of titanic importance in New York architecture and society in the 19th century. When the Municipal Art Society (of which Hunt was the founding president) erected its beautiful memorial to Hunt, they selected the west side of Fifth Avenue between 70th and 71st Streets so the memorial would look across the avenue to one of Hunt's most famous buildings. The best laid plans....

The Frick is an old-fashioned museum – with an impressive book store. Bear in mind that children under ten are not permitted.

THE METROPOLITAN MUSEUM OF ART

Fifth Avenue and 82nd Street
Built 1894-1902
Architects: Richard Morris Hunt (1827-1895) and Richard Howland Hunt (1862-1931)
Architects of 1904-1926 extensions: McKim, Mead & White
Architects of 1970s and 1980s extensions: Kevin Roche John Dinkeloo & Associates

The Met is the great encyclopedic art museum of the Western Hemisphere. Within its walls can be found the full range of artistic expression from ancient times to the present, spanning the entire globe. For many New Yorkers, it is the one thing above all others without which New York would be unthinkable.

Even the most cursory summary of the Met's departments would take up too much space, but highlights include the Greek and Roman galleries, the Egyptian collection, European paintings, and the American Wing. The Lehman Wing is a museum-within-the-museum, as it keeps together in its own wing the many diverse objects from one of the greatest private collections in New York.

The Met opened in its Central Park location in 1880 after it had spent its earliest years moving from place to place as the collections grew. Still, the museum was not world-class until the great banker and collector J.P. Morgan became its president in 1904. The original Victorian Gothic building (a wall of which can still be seen inside the Lehman Wing) had been twice expanded (a wall of the first addition is still visible in the Petrie European Sculpture Court) and the majestic central section was already in place on Fifth Avenue opposite East 82nd Street. That section was designed by Richard Morris Hunt, the first American (of what would be many) to attend the fabled Ecole des Beaux-Arts in Paris. Under Morgan, the architects McKim, Mead & White added the long north and south wings. The grand staircase – a favorite place for New Yorkers and tourists alike to sit and watch the passing parade – was given its present appearance in a 1975 renovation by Kevin Roche John Dinkeloo & Associates, who also designed the five new wings (including the Lehman Wing) that radiate from the west side of the main building.

Unusual are the great heaps of uncarved stone sitting atop the entablatures supported by the paired Corinthian columns of the facade. Hunt intended that these masses of stone be carved into elaborate sculptural groups by Karl Bitter, who provided all the sculptural embellishment of the facade. But museum trustees, trying to rein in costs, put off the expense of carving – and we are still waiting.

Once up the stairs, the visitor enters into the Great Hall, one of the most breathtaking spaces in New York. We credit the design of this hall to Richard Howland Hunt, son of Richard Morris Hunt, who died while the museum was under construction. Another great

staircase leads to the second floor, where the European paintings are hung in beautifully designed galleries. At the top of the stairs is "The Triumph of Marius," an 18th-century masterpiece by the Venetian Giovanni Battista Tiepolo. It is one of the most exciting spots in New York – indeed, in America.

The museum is now open 7 days a week (closed Thanksgiving Day, December 25, January 1 and the first Monday in May.)

NEUE GALERIE

1048 Fifth Avenue at 86th Street
House built 1914, museum opened 2001
Architects of house: Carrère & Hastings
Architect of renovation: Annabelle Selldorf

In 1914, Carrère & Hastings (architects of the New York Public Library at 42nd Street) designed a house for the rich industrialist and real estate investor William Starr Miller at the southeast corner of Fifth Avenue and 86th Street. After Miller's death in 1935, Grace Wilson Vanderbilt, the wife of Cornelius Vanderbilt III and sister-in-law of Gertrude Vanderbilt Whitney (founder of the Whitney Museum of American Art), occupied the house. Later, and for many years, the house was home to the important YIVO Institute for Jewish Research, now housed in the Center for Jewish History at 15 West 16th Street. In 1994, Ronald Lauder and Serge Sabarsky purchased the house. Sabarsky had from 1968 to 1985 operated a Madison Avenue gallery that specialized in German and Austrian art of the late 19th and early 20th centuries. Lauder, born in 1944, is the son of Estée and Joseph Lauder, founders of the Estée Lauder Companies, famous for cosmetics. After working for the family business, Ronald Lauder was asked by President Ronald Reagan to be the United States Ambassador to Austria. Lauder was already in love with the late 19th and early 20th century art of Austria, and his and his friend Sabarsky's dream was to establish a New York museum dedicated to this art. Sabarsky died shortly after the two men bought the old mansion in which they planned to put their museum. So Lauder went it alone. The museum finally opened in November 2001 following an excellent renovation by the architect Annabelle Selldorf. The Neue Galerie immediately took its place among the museums of Manhattan's Museum Mile, along with the Metropolitan Museum of Art, the Guggenheim, the Jewish Museum, the Cooper-Hewitt, and others.

But the Neue Galerie became for a while *the* hottest attraction in New York when Lauder spent $135 million on a single, astonishing painting, *Adele Bloch-Bauer I*, by the Austrian Gustav Klimt. Painted in 1907, this mesmerizing portrait, notable for its gold background and intricate patterning, was commissioned from Klimt by Adele's husband, the industrialist Ferdinand Bloch-Bauer. In 1937, some years after his wife's death (in 1925 from meningitis), Bloch-Bauer, who was Jewish, fled Austria; his artworks were confiscated by the Nazis. After the war, the portrait of Adele became part of the Austrian national art collection and was exhibited in Vienna's Belvedere. For years, Bloch-Bauer's heirs tried to reclaim the painting. In 2006 Bloch-Bauer's niece, Maria Altmann, finally succeeded in the courts; she then, in June 2006, sold the painting to Lauder. At the time $135 million was the highest price ever paid for a painting. When,

soon after Lauder's purchase, the painting went on display at the Neue Galerie, lines blocks-long formed as art lovers – and curiosity seekers – came in droves to view the painting. It's hard to think of another phenomenon quite like it in New York's history. Today, two paintings (one by Jackson Pollock, one by Willem de Kooning) have sold for amounts greater than what Lauder paid for the Klimt. But don't go to see *Adele Bloch-Bauer I* because it is the most expensive painting in New York, go to

see it because it is one of the greatest paintings in New York.

It should be noted that Ronald Lauder has a longstanding interest in recovering art that was stolen by the Nazis. The Neue Galerie offers much more than one painting by Klimt displayed in a beautiful house. The exhibitions of German and Austrian art are always worth seeing. The museum also has a restaurant called Café Sabarsky, a creation of the renowned Austrian chef Kurt Gutenbrunner.

THE JEWISH MUSEUM

Fifth Avenue and 92nd Street
Built 1908. converted to museum 1947
Architect: C.P.H. Gilbert

The Jewish Museum contains the largest collection of art and cultural artifacts related to Jewish history and the Jewish experience of any museum in the world outside of Israel. The collection originated in 1904 at the Jewish Theological Seminary in Morningside Heights.

The Warburg house, built in 1908, is six stories, faced in limestone, and designed in an exuberant 15th-century French Gothic style, an essay in exotic fenestration, drip moldings, and crocketed finials etched against the sky. The architect, C.P.H. Gilbert, was one of the leading providers of grand (and sometimes grandiose) mansions to the Manhattan (and Brooklyn) elite, including the Joseph De Lamar mansion (now the Polish Consulate) on Madison Avenue and 37th Street. The building received an unsympathetic modern addition in 1963, but that was replaced by the architects Kevin Roche and John Dinkeloo in 1993 with an addition that perfectly (and controversially) matches the original house.

In 1947 the museum opened to the public, now housed in the former home of Frieda Schiff Warburg, who had donated it to the Seminary in 1944.

Frieda's late husband, Felix Moritz Warburg, was a member of the great banking family from Hamburg, Germany. He came to America to work for Kuhn, Loeb & Co., one of the most powerful banking houses on Wall Street, and married Frieda, daughter of the firm's head, Jacob Schiff.

From its beginning to the present day, the museum's purpose has been to present Jewish cultural artifacts from ancient times to the present day. In the 1950s and 1960s, the museum presented seminal exhibitions of contemporary art – including the first museum shows dedicated to Robert Rauschenberg and Jasper Johns – and became quite influential on the New York art scene. Recent exhibitions show the museum's remarkable scope: Harry Houdini: Art and Magic in 2010-11, Maira Kalman: Various Illustrations (of a Crazy World) in 2011, and Collecting Matisse and Modern Masters: The Cone Sisters of Baltimore in 2011. With such exhibitions, and a collection of more than 26,000 objects, the Jewish Museum has proudly taken its place in the heart of Museum Mile. The diversity of objects and diversity of aims has long made the Jewish Museum a uniquely exciting institution.

COOPER-HEWITT NATIONAL DESIGN MUSEUM (Andrew Carnegie Mansion)

2 East 91st Street
Built 1903
Architects: Babb, Cook & Willard

When Andrew Carnegie built his mansion at 2 East 91st Street in 1903, he had recently sold his Carnegie Steel Company to J.P. Morgan's new conglomerate, U.S. Steel. How rich did the sale make Carnegie? Well, historians reckon that Carnegie was the second richest American of all time. (John D. Rockefeller was the richest.) The Fifth Avenue mansion was where Carnegie would settle down (he had built his business in Pittsburgh, where the Scottish-born steel baron had grown up) and concentrate on his unprecedented philanthropies (from the Carnegie branch libraries built all across America to Carnegie Hall on 57th Street). Some people were surprised when Carnegie chose to build so far uptown, in an area that had none of the cachet of the neighborhoods ten or twenty blocks to the south. What Carnegie's chosen neighborhood did have, however, was space. Babb, Cook & Willard's marvelous house, in an English Georgian style, is, as one would expect, large and grand – and surrounded by lawns and gardens. But the house has an air of modesty – the modesty that only such a fabulous fortune could buy. Carnegie also bought up a number of nearby house lots and sold them for development,

and the neighborhood soon bore his name: Carnegie Hill.

When Carnegie died in 1919, ownership of the house passed to the Carnegie Corporation, the remarkable philanthropic foundation he had founded. In 1972, the Corporation donated the mansion to the Smithsonian Institution to house the Cooper-Hewitt National Design Museum. The Museum for the Arts of Decoration, as it was originally called, opened in 1897 as part of Cooper Union. (The museum became part of the Smithsonian in 1967.) The museum's extensive collections are divided into four curatorial departments: Drawings, Prints, & Graphic Design; Product Design & Decorative Arts; Textiles; and Wallcoverings. The museum also houses the 70,000-volume Doris and Henry Dreyfuss Study Center Library and Archive, sponsors the annual National Design Awards, and, in conjunction with Parsons School of Design, offers a Master of Arts degree in History of Decorative Arts and Design. Recent exhibitions have ranged from "Rococo: The Continuing Curve 1730-2008" in 2008 to "Set in Style: The Jewelry of Van Cleef & Arpels" in 2011.

SOLOMON R. GUGGENHEIM MUSEUM

Fifth Avenue and 89th Street
Built 1956-59
Architect: Frank Lloyd Wright

It is almost a truism to say that Frank Lloyd Wright is the greatest American architect. (He certainly thought he was.) Born in Wisconsin, where he maintained a home for most of his life, he began his career in booming Chicago, working for the great Louis Sullivan before setting up on his own in the leafy suburb of Oak Park, Illinois. There and in neighboring towns he injected his radical "Prairie style" houses among the conventional Victorian villas, and proceeded with each new decade of his long life to reinvent himself, building a spectacular home for himself in Arizona, working in Los Angeles, designing Tokyo's Imperial Hotel, prophesying the rise of suburbia (indeed, of 'exurbia'). Though he denounced New York ("the Moloch that knows no god but More"), he simply couldn't stay away. And he always stayed at the Plaza Hotel, which he never denounced but praised loftily, different as it was from the buildings he designed.

It was at the Plaza that Wright met with Solomon Robert Guggenheim, heir to a vast mining fortune and collector of "non-objective art," as he called it – abstract painting, to the rest of us. Guggenheim's Museum of Non-Objective Painting was on 54th Street, but he wanted something bigger and better, a

building that would itself be a critical part of the collection. "I want a temple of the spirit, a monument!" said Hilla Rebay, Guggenheim's close adviser and director of his museum. Guggenheim, Rebay, and Wright began planning the new museum in 1943. It eventually opened in 1959 – ten years after Guggenheim's death! Wright's radical great white funnel was made of poured-in-place concrete in a way that had never been done before. The design would have been startling anywhere, but on Fifth Avenue opposite Central Park it was as though Wright had indelibly stamped his ego on the city. In the country, Wright strove to design with nature. But in the city he professed to hate, he created a building that seemed to fight with everything around it.

Not all artists are pleased with the building – some say they hate it. This may be because many visitors come to see the building rather than the art on the walls. The building used experimental construction techniques, and maintaining the structure has proved difficult and costly. But for all that may be said against it, the Guggenheim is a great icon of the city, and the crowning building in the career of America's most illustrious architect.

RIVERSIDE PARK

72nd to 158th Streets, Riverside Drive to the Hudson River
Built: 1873-75, 1934-37
Architects: Frederick Law Olmsted (1873-75),
Clifton Lloyd and Gilmore D. Clarke (1934-37)

Frances Perkins (President Roosevelt's Secretary of Labor) recalled one day in 1914 when she was in a boat on the Hudson River with Robert Moses, then a 26-year-old dreamer. Moses waved his arm toward the West Side riverfront of Manhattan. "Couldn't this waterfront be the most beautiful thing in the world?" he said. At the time that waterfront was occupied by piers for oceangoing ships, docks for carfloats and barges and lighters that came in constant waves from New Jersey, by warehouses and factories and railroads. It was a place for work, not beauty. But in the 1930s he was able to achieve his dream with the "West Side Improvement", a vast Depression-era project that gave us the High Line and the West Side Highway, the Henry

Hudson Parkway and, not least, a near doubling of Riverside Park.

Riverside Park was originally laid out by Frederick Law Olmsted in 1873-75 as part of the same project that left us the lovely, sinuously curving (such a rarity in gridded Manhattan!) Riverside Drive (called Riverside Avenue before 1908). Riverside Park was mostly a kind of green buffer zone between the fine town houses (and later fine apartment houses) of Riverside Drive and the noisy, smoky waterfront.

In 1934-37, as part of his West Side Improvement, Moses added 148 acres to Olmsted's Riverside Park, which was designed by Moses's talented landscape architects, Clifton Lloyd and Gilmore D. Clarke. Here was the first of the master builder's waterfront esplanades, a long

pedestrian path where one could stand
at the railing and gaze dreamily at the
mighty Hudson, across to the beautiful
Palisades, or north to the majestic
man-made wonder known as the

George Washington Bridge.

The beautiful Henry Hudson
Parkway, the extension north of 72nd
Street of the West Side Highway, was
carefully integrated into the park. Most

194

remarkably, Moses and company built a traffic rotary for the Parkway at 79th Street. Here the traffic flows atop the roof of an arcaded circus enclosing a fountain. Through arched openings on its west side, pedestrians move through the circus to a restaurant, then to the riverfront esplanade and a marina with 105 slips for boats. Here, many houseboat dwellers live year-round.

CATHEDRAL OF ST JOHN THE DIVINE

Amsterdam Avenue and 112th Street
Built from 1892, dedicated 1941
Architects: Heins & LaFarge (1892-1911), Ralph Adams Cram (1911-41)

In 1888 a competition was held for the design of New York's new Episcopal cathedral. The firm of Heins & LaFarge won the competition with a bold Romanesque/Byzantine design for a cathedral of improbably large dimensions. On December 27, 1892, the cornerstone was laid in Morningside Heights. Over the next quarter century or so the neighborhood would become home to Columbia University, Riverside Church, Union Theological Seminary, Jewish Theological Seminary, and other educational and religious institutions that would give this part of Harlem its nickname of "Acropolis of New York." The cathedral, though still unfinished, was consecrated on April 19, 1911. At that time only the rear parts of the church – apse, choir, crossing, and two apsidal chapels – had been completed. Work continued, but in 1911 Heins & LaFarge were replaced as architects by Ralph Adams Cram. Remarkably, Cram convinced the cathedral board that Heins & LaFarge's Romanesque/Byzantine design, which had guided construction for nearly 20 years, should be scuttled, and Cram's new design, in a monumental Gothic style recalling the great cathedrals of Medieval Europe, adopted. And so between 1911 and 1941 (construction was suspended at the time of U.S. entry into World War II), St. John the Divine made a complete change of direction, and emerged as the

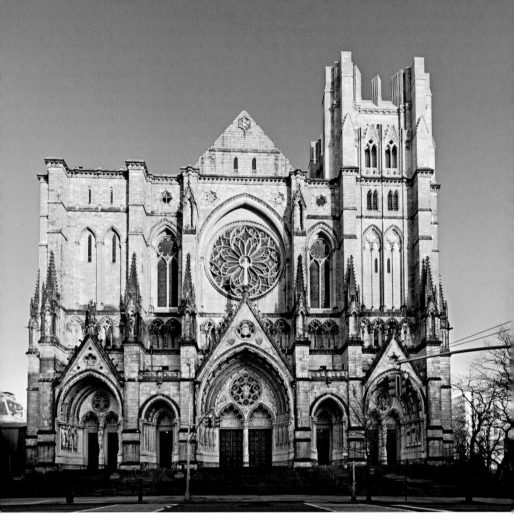

largest (though still unfinished) Gothic cathedral in the world. Today, the cathedral is still only about three quarters complete. Most work has been carried out using traditional methods, and like the cathedrals of the Middle Ages, St. John's is being built in fits and starts. Between 1982 and 1994 a fresh round of construction was undertaken in which, in an innovative program, young people from the surrounding Harlem neighborhood were trained in traditional stone carving techniques, under the direction of a master mason from England, and actually produced the finely carved stonework of the southwest tower. In 1982, just as this round of work commenced, the French aerialist Philippe Petit crossed Amsterdam Avenue on a high wire to hand Bishop Paul Moore a silver trowel on the roof of the cathedral. The interior richly rewards a visit. And be sure to look at Charles Connick's Great West Rose Window, the largest stained-glass window in America.

RIVERSIDE CHURCH

Riverside Drive and 120th Street
Built 1926-30
Architects: Henry C. Pelton (1868-1935) and Charles Collens (1873-1956)

John D. Rockefeller Jr. donated a substantial sum of money toward the construction of the Cathedral of St. John the Divine, but when he realized the Episcopal cathedral was not going to be as ecumenical as he had hoped, he decided he needed to build his own great church, one that would be truly interdenominational and dedicated to progressive social causes. And almost as though to show up St. John the Divine, which remains unfinished after 110 years, Rockefeller completed his enormous church in only a few years.

Riverside Church – dubbed "Rockefeller Cathedral" by the *New Yorker* magazine – rises majestically beside the Hudson River on Morningside Heights, near Columbia University. Viewed from a boat in the river, the church dominates this part of Manhattan. Not only is it built on a high elevation, but the church tower rises 392 feet – the highest church tower in America. Unlike the towers of St. Patrick's Cathedral, the single tower of Riverside is a full-fledged skyscraper, filled with offices, classrooms, and other practical spaces. At its top is the Laura Spelman Rockefeller Memorial Carillon, one of its 74 bronze bells is, at 20 tons, the largest tuned bell ever cast.

The style of the church is French Gothic, heavily inspired by Chartres Cathedral in France. When the church opened, Rockefeller installed Harry Emerson Fosdick in its pulpit. Fosdick was one of the most famous clergymen of his day, known for his liberal social views and ecumenical theology. The church has ever since been noted for its dedication to social justice, its racial diversity, and its many outreach programs in the Harlem community – and also for the majesty of its Gothic architecture.

APOLLO THEATER

253 West 125th Street
Built 1914
Architect: George Keister

The legendary Apollo Theater on 125th Street, the main commercial crosstown thoroughfare of Harlem, opened in 1914 as Hurtig & Seamon's New Burlesque Theater, one among a number of theaters that had made Harlem a center of burlesque. From 1928 to 1932 the theater was operated by Billy Minsky, of the family that ran a circuit of burlesque houses and made their name almost synonymous with the genre. Burlesque was a type of variety show popular in the late 19th and early 20th centuries. The shows featured "striptease artistes" (as they were called, and who were in fact considerably more artistic than modern-day "strippers"), novelty acts, and off-color humor. They were scandalous in their day, but seem quite tame by today's standards. Today there is a revival of interest in old-time burlesque, both in the downtown performance scene and in mainstream culture (the 2010 film *Burlesque* starring Cher and Christina Aguilera, for instance). But the Apollo, so named in 1934 by new owners Frank Schiffman

and Leo Brecher, became legendary for something else. "Amateur Night at the Apollo," inaugurated in 1934, as well as other performances showcased (and continue to showcase) the best in African-American performing arts. And, unlike some of the clubs that became famous during the Harlem Renaissance of the 1920s, the Apollo catered to an African-American audience. The audience on Amateur Night could be wildly enthusiastic or mercilessly dismissive, and in its discernment helped launch the careers of Ella Fitzgerald (who, at 17, made her debut at the Apollo in 1934), Billie Holiday, Sarah Vaughan, Nancy Wilson, Aretha Franklin, James Brown, Stevie Wonder, Marvin Gaye, and Michael Jackson – just to name a few. After a phase of decline in the 1970s that saw the Apollo converted to a movie theater, in 1983 Inner City Broadcasting brought the Apollo back to life, Amateur Night and all. Today, following restoration and designation as a city landmark, the Apollo is going as strong as ever.

STRIVERS' ROW

*138th and 139th Streets between Adam Clayton Powell Jr. Boulevard and
Frederick Douglass Boulevard
Built 1891-93
Architects: McKim, Mead & White, Bruce Price, Clarence Luce, James Brown Lord*

Between 1891 and 1893 a real-estate developer named David King built a group of 146 row houses and three apartment houses on West 138th and 139th Streets between Adam Clayton Powell Jr. Boulevard (Seventh Avenue) and Frederick Douglass Boulevard (Eighth Avenue). At that time, Harlem was being developed as what builders presumed would be the next upper-middle-class or upper-class enclave in Manhattan. King called his project the "King Model Houses" – a "model" in that this was an unusually large and harmonious and carefully designed group of houses. Typical Manhattan row house streets, let alone several continuous blockfronts, were seldom built by the same developer. And while lot sizes and the prevailing taste did lead to uniformity – or harmony – on many of the city's row house streets, the King Model Houses were different. These houses are essays in elegant brickwork, subtle, meticulous Italian Renaissance-style detailing, and fine ironwork. King brought in some of the city's best architects, including McKim, Mead & White, Bruce Price, Clarence Luce, and James Brown Lord. But what happened to Harlem as a whole happened to the King Model Houses. Speculative overbuilding meant that

houses stood vacant. That's when Philip Payton, an African-American realtor, promoted the idea that Harlem's houses and apartments be marketed to African-Americans, many of whom would jump at the opportunity to live in such fine housing but had been deterred from doing so. And so Harlem became black, and with it the King Model Houses, which came to be known as "Strivers' Row" – home to upwardly mobile, "striving" African-Americans. Residents of the houses over the years included many celebrities, such as Eubie Blake, Congressman Adam Clayton Powell Jr., Bill "Bojangles" Robinson, and W.C. Handy. Spike Lee's 1991 film *Jungle Fever* starring Wesley Snipes was filmed there. Please note: These are not "brownstones." Most of New York's row houses were built between 1800 and 1900. Until about 1850 almost all row houses were red brick. Then it became fashionable for houses to be faced in a local brown sandstone. These dominated the second half of the 19th century, and only they should be called "brownstones." Other row houses are of white limestone or, as here, golden brick (with brownstone bases). These should just be called "row houses." Or, at Strivers' Row, they should be called very beautiful row houses.

THE CLOISTERS

Fort Tryon Park, Broadway and Dyckman Street
Built 1938
Architect: Charles Collens (1873-1956)

When John D. Rockefeller Jr. built his monumental Riverside Church (see page 198), his choice of the Gothic style suggested his fondness for the Middle Ages. When a few years later he gave us the Cloisters, high on the hill of Fort Tryon Park in upper Manhattan, he showed that he was, in fact, obsessed with the Middle Ages. This remarkable museum of Medieval antiquities, including several cloisters from European monasteries, is today a department of the Metropolitan Museum of Art and is one of the most

remarkable museums in the world.

The story starts with an American sculptor named George Gray Barnard. Barnard lived in France for a number of years, and began to collect Medieval art, including cloisters that, in the various religious conflicts over the centuries, had been emptied or ruined. He shipped all of these to New York where he established his own museum, called Barnard's Cloisters, on Fort Washington Avenue and 190th Street. When after some years he was strapped for cash, his friend, the architect Welles Bosworth,

persuaded his client, Rockefeller (Bosworth designed the Rockefeller mansion, Kykuit, in Tarrytown, New York), to pay Barnard a visit. Rockefeller bought the collection. He then bought the old estate of a rich Manhattanite named C.K.G. Billings, tore down Billings's mansion, and hired Frederick Law Olmsted Jr. (the exceptionally talented son of the co-designer of Central Park) to turn the estate's hilly location into a beautiful park.

At the crest of the hill Rockefeller had Charles Collens, the architect of Riverside Church, design a setting for Barnard's collection, which was supplemented by items from Rockefeller's own collection (including the famous Unicorn Tapestries, which had been hanging in the Rockefellers' West 54th Street town house). To ensure that the majestic view across the Hudson River would never be spoiled, Rockefeller bought several hundred acres of New Jersey's riverfront palisades. He then transferred ownership of the palisades acreage to the State of New Jersey, and of Fort Tryon Park to the City of New York. The Cloisters opened in 1938, a testament to what one very determined (and very rich) man can achieve.

GEORGE WASHINGTON BRIDGE

Connecting West 178th Street to Fort Lee, New Jersey, across the Hudson River
Built 1927-31
Engineer: Othmar Hermann Ammann

The George Washington Bridge was from 1931 to 1937 the world's longest suspension bridge, replaced by the Golden Gate. It surpassed the Ambassador Bridge, connecting Detroit with Windsor, Ontario, the main span of which it exceeded by 1,650 feet, or by more than the length of the Brooklyn Bridge. (It exceeded the length of New York's longest suspension bridge, the Williamsburg Bridge, by 1,900 feet, or by well more than twice.) And although the George Washington would remain the world's longest suspension bridge for only six years, and is no longer even the longest in New York, its legend, which will never diminish, resides in the fact that no bridge in history (not even the Brooklyn Bridge) took such a leap

forward. There had never been a bridge with even a 2,000-foot main span when the George Washington came in at 3,500. It inaugurated the age of the super-long bridge. And in one important respect it remains number one: The George Washington Bridge carries more vehicular traffic than any other bridge in the world. The bridge also has more vehicular lanes – fourteen – than any other bridge. In 1962, in accordance with original plans, a lower level roadway was added. New Yorkers immediately dubbed the lower lane "Martha." The bridge's designer, the Swiss-born Othmar Hermann Ammann (1879-1965), had few rivals among 20th-century bridge designers. His credits include twice designing the world's longest bridge – the George Washington and the Verrazano-Narrows (1964). He also designed the Bronx-Whitestone, Triborough, Throgs Neck, and many other major bridges. He lived at the top of the Carlyle Hotel on Madison Avenue, in an apartment with views in three directions, so he could look out on his creations. Under the bridge, just off the Manhattan shoreline, has stood since 1921 the charming, squat, red-painted Jeffrey's Hook Lighthouse, immortalized in the 1942 children's classic *The Little Red Lighthouse and the Great Gray Bridge* by Hildegarde Swift and Lynd Ward.

YANKEE STADIUM

River Avenue and 161st Street, Bronx
Built 2009
Architect: Populous

The New York Yankees, love 'em or hate 'em, are the most storied franchise in the history of professional sports in America. The franchise dates back to the New York Highlanders who played in upper Manhattan from 1903. In 1913 the team changed its name to the Yankees, and from that year to 1922 shared the ballpark known as the Polo Grounds with the New York Giants. The Yankees won their first American League pennant in 1921 (they lost the World Series to their parkmates the Giants) after acquiring Babe Ruth from the Boston Red Sox. Ruth, a pitcher turned outfielder, quickly established himself as by far and away the game's most dominant player, and glory years ensued for the Yankees, who, in 1923, won the first of their eventual 27 World Series championships. In that year, the team moved across the Harlem River to the Bronx, to the "House That Ruth Built," also known as Yankee Stadium. That stadium became sports' most legendary venue, home to greats such as Lou Gehrig, Joe DiMaggio, Mickey Mantle, Reggie Jackson, and Derek Jeter. In 1973, when the Yankees were, uncharacteristically, a struggling franchise, the team was purchased by Cleveland businessman George Steinbrenner. He arranged for a lavish, city-funded renovation of Yankee Stadium, completed in 1974. Soon thereafter the Yankees resumed their winning ways. But by the first decade of the 21st century, the Yankees felt the need

of an entirely new facility, and between 2006 and 2009 a new Yankee Stadium rose across the street from the old one. Its stately classical design, with an exterior of Indiana limestone, draws heavily from the old stadium. The new

stadium actually seats slightly fewer people than the old one (a little more than 53,000 compared to almost 57,000), but has 56 state-of-the-art (and highly lucrative) "luxury suites," compared to the old 19. The Yankees, in their first year of occupancy of the new stadium, promptly won their 27th World Series, defeating the Philadelphia Phillies four games to two – just as they had won their first World Series in their first year in the old Yankee Stadium.

NEW YORK BOTANICAL GARDEN AND BRONX ZOO

2900 Southern Boulevard, Bronx
Founded 1891

The 250-acre New York Botanical Garden, located in Bronx Park, is the most important botanical garden in the United States. The Garden grew out of the Torrey Botanical Club, America's oldest botanical society, founded in the 1860s and dedicated to the study of New York-region flora. Two Torrey members, the husband and wife botanists Nathaniel Lord Britton and Elizabeth Gertrude Knight, founded the New York Botanical Garden in 1891. They wanted an American equivalent of the Royal Botanical Garden at Kew, England, which they had visited on their honeymoon. The Brittons secured donations from Cornelius Vanderbilt II, J.P. Morgan, and Andrew Carnegie, and engaged the redoubtable Calvert Vaux and Samuel Parsons Jr. to lay out the grounds. The Garden is located on part of the former estate of tobacco tycoon Pierre Lorillard, next to the Bronx Zoo (opened 1899). In few places in America are two attractions of such caliber located side by side, and any visitor to New York will be glad to take the trip to the Bronx to see them. The Garden

includes a 50-acre virgin forest, with some trees more than 200 years old, the largest remaining tract of the extensive forests that predated the European settlement of the region in the 17th century; the Peggy Rockefeller Rose Garden, laid out in 1916 by the great landscape gardener Beatrix Farrand; and the Pfizer Plant Research Laboratory, opened in 2006, a world-leading center of research in plant genomics. The Enid Annenberg Haupt Conservatory, built in 1899-1902, is one of the greatest greenhouses in America; its architects, Lord & Burnham, were the greatest greenhouse designers in America. Greenhouses require a great deal of upkeep, and the Haupt Conservatory was renovated in the 1990s by Beyer Blinder Belle. The Garden's vast main building, called simply the Museum Building, was built in 1899-1901 and designed by Robert W. Gibson. With its high Corinthian columns, shields in scroll frames, rusticated stonework, abundance of carved ornamentation, and Carl Tefft's dramatic Fountain of Life, it is one of the handful of the finest Beaux-Arts buildings in New York, alone worth the trip to the Bronx.

ARTHUR ASHE STADIUM & CITI FIELD

Flushing Meadows-Corona Park, Queens
Arthur Ashe Stadium built 1997, Citi Field built 2009
Architects: Rossetti Architects (Arthur Ashe Stadium), Populous (Citi Field)

In Flushing Meadows-Corona Park, built by Robert Moses on the site of an old ash dump (the "Valley of Ashes" described by F. Scott Fitzgerald in *The Great Gatsby*) in Queens, is, among much else, a great center of American sport. The center comprises the new stadium, Citi Field, of the National League New York Mets, and the lavish National Tennis Center, home to the U.S. Open, which many sporting enthusiasts regard as the greatest

annual event in American sports. Work on building the National Tennis Center in Flushing started in 1977 in the old Louis Armstrong Stadium. In 1978, the U.S. Open, which had been held since 1914 at the West Side Tennis Club in Forest Hills, Queens, moved to Flushing. Under New York's tennis-loving mayor David Dinkins, the new 22,000-seat Arthur Ashe Stadium was added to the Billie Jean King National Tennis Center in 1997. There is no more exciting place in America to watch the game, especially over the Labor Day

weekend when the U.S. Open takes over New York City.

The Mets were founded in 1962 following the defections to the West Coast of the Brooklyn Dodgers and New York Giants. That year, the Mets won 40 games and lost 120. In their first seven years the team did not come close to a winning record, and finished dead last in the league five times. New Yorkers took the team to their hearts precisely because they were so comically inept. Then, in one of the greatest surprises in baseball history, the Mets of 1969 caught fire and won the first of the team's two World Series titles. From 1964 to 2008 the Mets played in the old Shea Stadium. In 2000 the Mets lost to the Yankees in the first all-New York World Series since the Yankees defeated the Dodgers in 1956. In 2009, Citi Field opened, in the same year as the new Yankee Stadium. The two stadiums were both designed by the firm called Populous (formerly HOK Sport), the biggest stadium designers in the world.

BROOKLYN MUSEUM

200 Eastern Parkway, Brooklyn
Built 1893-1915, new front 2004
Architects: McKim, Mead & White, new front by Polshek Partnership

When McKim, Mead & White, perhaps the most prestigious architectural firm in the nation, won a competition to design the Brooklyn Museum, they proposed something that could be built in stages; the first part opened in 1897. But in 1898 Brooklyn merged with New York, and Brooklyn's desire to rival the Metropolitan Museum of Art was never realized. Today, the Brooklyn Museum is only about a fourth as large as planned. Even so, it is one of the world's largest museums. The Egyptian collection is of such

renown that most Egyptologists must, at some point in their careers, come to Brooklyn to study. From aboriginal artifacts of the Americas, to African tribal art, to American paintings (especially the Hudson River School landscape paintings) and watercolors (as fine a collection as there is in the country), the Brooklyn yields treasures not to be seen in any other New York museum. The building, which we credit to Charles Follen McKim, originally had a monumental stairway rising to the museum's third floor. This was removed in 1934-35, ostensibly to make the entryway appear less forbidding. In truth, it was as much a make-work project for unemployed laborers as anything else. In 2004, under director Arnold Lehman, a radical glass addition, designed by the Polshek Partnership, was placed on the front of the building. Some love the exciting contrast with McKim's limestone-clad classical museum. Others feel a flying saucer has crashed into the front of the building. Love it or hate it, no one who takes the train to Eastern Parkway to visit the Brooklyn Museum regrets the experience.

BROOKLYN BOTANIC GARDEN

Main entrance 1000 Washington Avenue
Built beginning in 1910
Architects of general layout: Olmsted Brothers

First things first: It is Brooklyn *Botanic*
Garden, but (in the Bronx) New York
Botanical Garden. (In both cases, it is
'Garden', singular.) The Brooklyn Botanic
Garden is the smallest of the world's
truly important botanical gardens. It's
but fifty-two acres, built on a former ash
dump. But the quality of its collections
and importance of its research and
publications are known worldwide. The
Garden contains some 13,000 species of
plants in thirteen specialized gardens.
Among these are the Local Flora Section,
begun in 1911 and comprising only plants
native to within 100 miles of the Botanic
Garden; the Cranford Rose Garden which
blooms in early summer with tens of
thousands of roses (nearly 1,400 varieties
of them); and the Cherry Esplanade, from
late March to mid-May by far the
Garden's most popular attraction when
the pink-petaled Kwanzan cherry trees
(the largest collection of Oriental
flowering cherries outside of Japan)
blossom so spectacularly (the trees were
first planted here in 1941). Another must-
see feature is the Japanese Hill-and-Pond
Garden, built in 1914-15. It was designed
by the Japanese landscape gardener
Takeo Shiota, who tragically died in an
internment camp in South Carolina in
1943. This is generally believed to be the
most authentic and beautiful Japanese
garden outside of Japan. With its pond,
hills, waterfall, island, bridges, teahouse,
torii, lanterns, shrine to the Shinto god
of the harvest, and more flowering

cherry trees, this is a "stroll garden," meant to be walked in, rather than a "viewing garden," meant to be contemplated from a stationary viewpoint, and is based on gardens of the Edo period (17th-19th centuries). And don't miss the Shakespeare Garden, the Fragrance Garden (designed by Alice Ireys, opened in 1955, and meant to be enjoyed by the blind), and, not least, the famous C.V. Starr Bonsai Museum, the largest bonsai collection outside of – you guessed it – Japan.

VERRAZANO-NARROWS BRIDGE & MARATHON

Connecting Bay Ridge, Brooklyn, to Staten Island, across the Narrows separating the Upper and Lower Bays of New York Harbor
Built 1964
Engineer: Othmar Hermann Ammann

When one flies into New York City, day or night, it is not the tall buildings that catch one's eye but the bridges, the majestic spans slung with otherworldly grace across the great waters that encircle the islands that make up the city. Of these bridges, the Brooklyn is the most historic, the George Washington the one that marked the greatest leap forward in bridge construction. Four of the New York bridges once held the title of world's longest suspension bridge. Another, the Robert F. Kennedy Bridge (formerly the Triborough), may be the most complex feat of bridge construction in history. Down there, it's a world of superlatives. More

important, it's a visual spectacle as dazzling as anything in the world. And in many ways the most dazzling of the bridges is the Verrazano-Narrows Bridge. From its completion in 1964 to 1981 it was the longest suspension bridge in the world; its main span of 4,260 feet exceeded that of the Golden Gate Bridge (1937) by sixty feet. It yielded its title to the Humber Bridge in England, and today, ranks number eight in the world. (The world's longest today is the Akashi Kaikyō Bridge in Japan.) The Verrazano, named for the 16th-century Florentine master mariner who, in the service of King Francis I of France, is believed to be the first European to sail his ship into New York Harbor, was the first bridge for which the engineers had to take into account the curvature of the earth. The Verrazano is also known to the world for its role in one of New York's most famous annual events. When the first New York Marathon was held in 1970, its 26.2-mile course consisted of laps around Central Park. Today, the course is designed to touch down in each of the five boroughs. The great race begins on Staten Island, near the entrance to the Verrazano Bridge, which is closed to vehicular traffic for the occasion. Then, all of a sudden, tens of thousands of runners cross the bridge. It is a sight like no other.

INDEX OF ARCHITECTS, DESIGNERS AND ENGINEERS